Praise
American

T0244631

A *Washington Post* Most Anticipated Title

"Sergeant Aquilino Gonell's story—of coming to America as a child, of overcoming adversity and discrimination, of stepping forward to defend democracy, of refusing to stay silent in the face of injustice—is riveting. It was moving to read about his first visit to the United States Capitol as a student, marveling at the majesty of the Dome and in awe of its hallowed halls. Decades later, it was there at the Capitol where he would display extraordinary heroism on January 6: recalling in raw and harrowing detail how he endured unimaginable brutality and lasting trauma, only to see many of those he risked his life to protect minimize that dark day. Our nation owes a debt of gratitude to Sergeant Gonell for his courageous and continued service, speaking out to ensure that we all remember the truth of the insurrection. *American Shield* is an all-American tale of duty and determination—beautifully told by an immigrant, a veteran, and a patriot."

—NANCY PELOSI, Speaker Emerita of the
United States House of Representatives

"Whenever duty calls, Sergeant Gonell answers. His story of service and resilience is uplifting and inspiring. And he's my height, which I also admire!"   —JON STEWART

"If you want to know what it was really like to face the mob of insurrectionists on January 6, and the overwhelming odds facing police that day, this very personal, very powerful memoir is essential reading. And if you want to know what courage looks like—in Iraq, on the steps of the Capitol, or risking it all again by speaking out to millions—it looks a lot like the strong, proud, unassuming, and brave countenance of an immigrant and U.S. sergeant named Aquilino Gonell."

—CONGRESSMAN ADAM SCHIFF

"To journey to America and fight for your piece of the American Dream is one thing. To then take an oath to help others in a foreign land get a piece of their own freedom is courageous. To come home from war and take *another* oath only to find yourself defending that freedom against your fellow Americans is a nightmare—one that some involved on January 6 have not yet awakened from. *American Shield* is a tale of how to survive the battles we choose and the battles that choose us."

—Roy Wood Jr., *The Daily Show*

"Sergeant Aquilino Gonell is a national hero and a patriot who put his life at risk in the line of duty to serve our nation and defend our democracy. He took an oath to protect our nation against all enemies, foreign and domestic, and stood on the frontlines amid the threats of the January 6 insurrection and the direct assault on our Capitol, the Congress, and more important, the Constitution. Sergeant Gonell is a patriot and has defended our nation valiantly, and I am honored to call him a friend, a brother, a fellow Dominican, and a hero. I commend him for sharing his story, which is a part of American history, with each of us."

—Congressman Adriano Espaillat

"This modern America makes it hard sometimes to find the will to believe. Vicious nativism, worsening radicalization, and poisonous white supremacy confront us every day with real and pressing dangers. But Aquilino Gonell's story is a redemption we probably don't deserve. For an immigrant to defend this nation on January 6 against those very forces, to navigate one American folly after another, is more than enough to rekindle the flames of belief again. Read this book and fight to rediscover faith once more."

—Jared Yates Sexton, author of *The Midnight Kingdom*

"Sgt. Aquilino Gonell's story is that of a true American patriot. A life dedicated to the service of his country. It was my honor to serve alongside him in the Lower West Terrace Tunnel on January 6, 2021."

—Michael Fanone

AMERICAN
SHIELD

The Immigrant Sergeant
Who Defended Democracy

AQUILINO GONELL
and SUSAN SHAPIRO

PREFACE BY CONGRESSMAN JAMIE RASKIN

COUNTERPOINT
CALIFORNIA

American Shield

First Counterpoint edition: 2023
First paperback edition: 2024

The Library of Congress has cataloged the hardcover edition as follows:
Names: Gonell, Aquilino, author. | Shapiro, Susan, author.
Title: American shield : the immigrant sergeant who defended democracy /
    Aquilino Gonell, and Susan Shapiro ; preface by Congressman Jamie Raskin
Description: First Counterpoint edition. | Berkeley, California : Counterpoint,
    2023.
Identifiers: LCCN 2023018980 | ISBN 9781640096288 (hardcover) | ISBN
    9781640096295 (ebook)
Subjects: LCSH: Capitol Riot, Washington, D.C., 2021. | Gonell, Aquilino.
    | United States. Capitol Police—Biography. | Political violence—
    Washington (D.C.)—History—21st century. | Riots—Washington
    (D.C.)—History—21st century. | Demonstrations—Washington (D.C.)—
    History—21st century. | Dominican Americans—New York (State)—New
    York—Biography.
Classification: LCC E915.G66 G66 2023 | DDC 973.933 [B]—dc23/
    eng/20230428
LC record available at https://lccn.loc.gov/2023018980

Paperback ISBN: 978-1-64009-667-7

Cover design by Nicole Caputo

COUNTERPOINT
Los Angeles and San Francisco, CA
www.counterpointpress.com

Printed in the United States of America
10 9 8 7 6 5 4 3 2 1

In loving memory of my grandfather Fillo
and for my wife, Monica, and our son, Emmanuel,
Dios los bendiga.

CONTENTS

PREFACE

This Is How You Pronounce *Patriot*

by Congressman Jamie Raskin

WHEN FUTURE GENERATIONS COME TO TELL THE story of the violent insurrection and attempted coup at the United States Capitol on January 6, 2021, and of the sharp social disparities, political corruption, and ideological fanaticisms that set the stage for this catastrophe, the spotlight will, of necessity, shine on the disgraced and twice-impeached ex-president Donald Trump: the pathological liar, narcissist, and con man who set all of the relevant events into motion and ruthlessly incited the bloody mob violence that shook America to the core.

But who will become the symbol of the besieged American democracy that fought back with vigor and honor at every turn, narrowly defeating a violent and unlawful seizure of the presidency outside of the constitutional order?

It just might be the unlikely figure of former Capitol Police Sergeant Aquilino Gonell, an immigrant from the Dominican Republic and naturalized citizen with a thick accent, a U.S. army veteran who fought in the Iraq war (no bone spurs) and then joined the Capitol Police, where he served honorably for sixteen years before he was badly wounded in the January 6 riot and forced to leave the force.

This remarkable little book tells the life of a man who is billionaire Trump's absolute opposite in nearly every respect.

Born into a large, destitute family in the countryside of the Dominican Republic, Aquilino learned a ferocious and honest work ethic from an early age, taking jobs stocking groceries at a bodega and selling his beloved mother's food door-to-door in impoverished neighborhoods.

Aquilino did share something in common with Donald Trump: he also had a mean son-of-a-bitch as a father. But where Trump came to identify completely with his racist cheat of an old man, Aquilino rebelled early against his father's constant domestic slights, aggressions, and betrayals. Trump's character weakness made him a hateful authoritarian bully. Aquilino's character strength made him a man of courage, respect, and honor, all the makings of a true patriot.

When Aquilino's family moved to New York City, he was a tiny little fish out of water: a shy immigrant kid who could not speak English, was falling behind in school, badly missed his revered grandfather and family back in the Dominican Republic, worked to make money for his family all the time, and despaired of having any real future in the urban jungle of New York City or the still-distant dream of America.

But Aquilino had something that marked him for happiness and growth in this world: a love of learning and education, even against all the odds stacked up around him like tenement buildings.

He connected with one of his teachers who pulled him up out of the doldrums and taught him painstakingly how to pronounce the word *patriot*. She also sent him on a class trip to the nation's capital, where he would meet a Capitol Police officer who would plant in him the seeds of a career ambition.

Aquilino became the first person in his family ever to graduate from high school. He wanted to go to college, which was not in the cards financially for him—until he learned about the possibility of joining the U.S. army and getting some of his tuition paid for. He also learned that he could become a naturalized citizen through his army service.

This is how he ended up in Iraq, getting an intense education in military bureaucracy, the democratic and humane impulses of America's young people, the cruel folly of imperial war, and the corruption and deceit of a lot of politicians.

Returning from war, he went to college, still struggling with his thick Dominican accent, but ended up in his American dream job serving as an officer on the Capitol Police.

It never could have occurred to him that his decorated career as a Capitol cop would end with injuries suffered in the worst violent insurrection at the Capitol in American history.

Aquilino experienced more brutal violence in Washington than he ever saw in Baghdad. When he testified before the Select Committee to Investigate the January 6th Attack on the United States Capitol, he famously described the experience of fighting a rampaging mob of Trump supporters for hours to defend the Capitol, the Members of Congress, and the Vice President as akin to participating in "medieval combat," an image that swept the country and was borrowed from him by President Joe Biden.

But I will let him tell you the full bloody story of the day he thought was going to be his last on earth. He and his brothers-in-arms—Capitol Police Officer Harry Dunn of Maryland's beautiful 8th District, Metropolitan Police Officer Michael Fanone, and Officer Daniel Hodges, who was tortured before the entire world in the Capitol doorway by an insurrectionist—have not just a right but a duty to tell the world the stories of what they barely lived through on that day we almost lost American democracy.

What you need to know is that there is beautiful life-affirming magic in this book, and we all owe Sergeant Gonell, his wife, Monica, and his justly proud son a debt of gratitude and solidarity.

Aquilino Gonell's name is tough to pronounce, but it sounds to me a lot like the word *patriot*.

AMERICAN
‒SHIELD‒

PROLOGUE

Never Tell Lies

Washington, D.C., December 2022

THE LAST THING I EVER WANTED TO BE WAS A troublemaker.

As I grew up in the Dominican Republic, my grandparents taught me to keep quiet. With no dad around, I listened when Abuelo Bienvenido, Mom's father, told me "Speak only when you're spoken to." He had thirteen kids and eight grandkids. I wasn't his favorite. To win him over, I said "Sí, Señor," and fed all the animals on his fruit and vegetable farm where we lived. Mom was a maid for a well-off family, then sold *frituras* on the street. I carried wood to the firepit and babysat my little brother and sister. All I ever hoped to be was useful and someone who made my family proud.

"Never tell lies," said my other grandfather, Fillo. Although he had seven kids and four grandkids, he treated me special. Not so his wife. When I was ten, Grandma Andrea told a neighbor, "We have no food to sell today." Knowing we did, I said, "Yes we do." She smacked my mouth, snapping, "Shut up, nobody's speaking to you." Later she yelled, "She owes us money. Don't contradict me. If you're not asked, keep your mouth closed." Lesson learned: let others do the talking.

Although my folks separated weeks after my birth and Dad wasn't around for my childhood, he resurfaced when I was twelve. He wanted us to be a family again and paid for Mom, my brother Tony, and me to join him in Brooklyn. I was excited to live with both parents and move to the States, but it wasn't as easy as I expected. Dad was a cabdriver, busy working all the time. I helped out as a stock boy at a bodega and sold Mom's food door to door. I gave my parents most of the cash I made, though not all. One morning, seeing my flashy new Nikes, Dad asked, "Why spend so much on that crap? What was wrong with the shoes I got you?" I felt ashamed. First rule from my father: be modest and blend in.

That was hard without speaking the language in America. My accent was heavy. I struggled, pronouncing "v" as "b," saying "berry" instead of "very." My teacher wasn't sympathetic. Once, when I asked her to repeat a word I missed, she gave me detention for being disruptive. I didn't want to disrupt anyone, so I stopped raising my hand. As a minority student and an immigrant, I couldn't risk calling attention to myself. I lived with the constant fear that something I did would get us deported.

Staying seen but not heard proved to be a good strategy. I became the first in my family to graduate high school. To afford college, I enlisted in the army. A team player, I saluted and obeyed the chain of command, waiting for permission to speak. I followed orders, replying "Yes, sir" when told to serve food at chow hall and clean barracks. My efforts kept paying off. I was honored to become a U.S. citizen and continue my service. The military was perfect training for joining the Capitol Police in Washington, D.C. For sixteen years, ordered to check ID, I checked. Sent to guard a dignitary's arrival, I guarded. I was cautious and careful as I moved up the ranks, rarely challenging higher-ups.

Though police unions nationwide endorsed Donald Trump, I was stunned to hear him call Black nations "shithole countries" and Mexican migrants "criminals, drug dealers, and rapists." "Trump doesn't mean what he says," a white supervisor said. "He's just joking." Trump didn't have my vote, but I kept my views to myself, reminding my squad we protected everyone equally. When he won the presidency, I worried. Traveling with my young son, whose English was better than mine, I noticed condescending stares, as if strangers found me less American for speaking Spanish. Or the wrong kind of foreigner (unlike Melania Trump's white Slovenian parents, who were naturalized through the kind of "chain migration" her husband vehemently denounced). Still, I stayed subdued. If someone confronted me, I'd say I was a veteran and show my police badge to avoid a fight.

Silence—the blueprint I'd relied on—became impossible on January 6, 2021. On that day, I was attacked while defending the Capitol against invasion by tens of thousands in a barbaric mob of rioters incited by President Trump. Swarms of assailants beat me—and my colleagues—with poles, sticks, broken pipes, and pieces of furniture. It was worse than combat I'd seen in Iraq. Holding the police line through hours of torture, bloody from fending off multiple rioters, I was called "un-American" and a traitor who broke his oath and deserved to be executed. Trampled from both sides, I thought: *This is how I'm going to die.*

Nine people did end up dead. I was so badly wounded that even after two surgeries I wasn't sure if I could do my job or take the lieutenant promotion I'd strived for. Instead of denouncing the siege and upholding the law, many of the Republican lawmakers I risked my life to shield did the unthinkable: they defended the former president and the insurrectionists, claiming the violent uprising by armed militia was "legitimate public discourse" and a "peaceful protest" conducted by "patriots."

As a public servant for two decades, I was horrified to hear the invaders painted as victims and felt compelled to tell my story. But my wife and I were petrified that Trump's influence could harm our family. So I kept my mouth shut. Then Harry Dunn, a Black colleague of thirteen years who was also traumatized by the attempted coup, spoke out. He exposed the violence and racist epithets hurled at him by the pro-Trump white nationalists who stormed the Capitol. In TV interviews, he revealed how he was berated and racially profiled by fellow U.S. citizens whose crimes were rationalized and concealed.

I identified with Dunn, another policeman of color, vilified for doing his job. I waited for the Republican leaders Lindsey Graham, Kevin McCarthy, Steve Scalise, Ted Cruz, Josh Hawley, and Marco Rubio—people I'd met and protected—to condemn the revolt. Yet they refused to blame our lawless ex-president for causing this historic tragedy. Hawley actually raised his fist in support of the rioters and printed the image on a cup for sale on his website.

Meanwhile, doctors and physical therapists kept trying to fix my chronic pain, recurring nightmares, and PTSD. One day, recovering from shoulder and foot surgery for injuries sustained in the attack, my leg elevated to keep the swelling down, I turned on the news to learn that the GOP had blocked a bipartisan probe of the January 6 insurrection. Then I saw Harry Dunn and his fellow officer Michael Fanone with two women, the mother and fiancée of Brian Sicknick, the forty-two-year-old officer who died from a stroke a day after fighting the rioters. The foursome went door to door in the U.S. Senate buildings to get support for an investigation into the dangerous ambush. It could have been my wife, son, mom, and dad begging our lawmakers to investigate the same mob who almost killed me.

After keeping quiet for decades, I lost it. I couldn't believe what cowards these politicians were. Shocked, I told my wife, "They pretend to support law enforcement while covering up what happened for their own political gain!"

My faith in the U.S. justice system capsized. I'd put everything on the line as a soldier and policeman to defend our democracy. I recalled the saying John F. Kennedy quoted: "All it takes for evil to triumph is for good men to do nothing" and the advice from activist and congressman John Lewis to get into "good trouble." I could no longer stay silent. An American proud of the sacrifices I made for our nation, I deserved a voice. To hell with not being disruptive. I was going public. I asked Harry Dunn to connect me with CNN. On June 3, 2021, I gave an interview. It was draining to relive the terrifying trauma that haunted me, but afterward an immense weight lifted. I was risking my job and the security of my family, but the truth was more important.

At forty-one, I left my comfort zone and spoke out—to my bosses, the district attorney, the FBI, before Congress, in *The New York Times* and *The Washington Post* and on Telemundo. I blew every whistle, testified to each horror I saw, and called out all the injustices I witnessed, regardless of whether the liars taunted, outnumbered, or outranked me. I was betrayed by the president of the United States. The obedient, scared little boy from *el campo* was gone. It was time to stand up to any authority who abused their power.

This is the story of how I stopped being afraid.

PART
ONE

1

Uncharted Land

Brooklyn, March 1992

I'D BEEN IN AMERICA ONLY TWO WEEKS WHEN I WOKE up to the sound of someone screaming "Help, help" from outside. It was my father. He'd been stabbed.

"Quilo and Tony! Quick, rush downstairs. Your dad's being held up!" my mother, Sabina, yelled in Spanish, tying a robe over her nightgown and rushing to the door.

"*Ya voy Mami!*" I called back, terrified and shivering.

It was one in the morning. My older brother and I had been sleeping on the lumpy burgundy couch in the living room. For a moment, I forgot where I was. At twelve, everything in this country still felt upside down. Following Tony, I jumped up to look out the window of our small Crown Heights walk-up. It took a few seconds to spot the brown jacket my father, Jose, wore to drive his livery taxi and to figure out that the shadowy body lying on the street bleeding was *mi papi*.

Shocked and operating on autopilot, I hurried to copy Tony and put on shoes and clothes. He grabbed our baseball bats, though we'd never hit anyone before. We trailed Mom down two flights of stairs. Inches of muddy snow covered the ground. We were freezing but buzzing from adrenaline, palms sweaty. Lights flashed on. Neighbors cried out. My father moaned in a pool of red slush. I'd only seen snow for the first time earlier that day, happy to be playing outside in the fun white powder. Now my heart shattered, watching Mom fall to the wet ground where I'd been playing just hours earlier. Lying next to Dad, she begged, *"Ayúdenme para que no muera"*—help me so we don't lose him.

"Jose from apartment C6 was stabbed!" the third-floor neighbor screamed out his window.

"I called the cops," shouted my cousin Modesto, who lived above us. "They're on their way."

"The thieves crossed Rochester Avenue," yelled a woman two flights above us, pointing.

My brother and Modesto joined a group of men chasing the two culprits who had knifed my father until they disappeared. Within minutes, three squad cars pulled up to our building. A policeman in a blue uniform surveyed the scene, his hand touching the gun on his holster. He called for help on his radio. After the ambulance carted Dad to the hospital, he approached my mother.

"You all right, ma'am?" he asked.

Sobbing, she could hardly talk, mumbling only *"que no se muera"*—don't let him die. Seeing she didn't understand English, he asked someone who spoke Spanish to question us about what happened while another policeman cordoned off the area with yellow tape. I couldn't figure out what was happening, but I was struck by how polite the officers were. Back home, we were more afraid of *la policia* than the bad guys.

It was hard to trust law enforcement in the Dominican Republic. Once, on a visit, my father went into the city to exchange dollars for pesos. The police were in cahoots with the money exchangers, who'd slipped a counterfeit $50 bill into Dad's stack. He was accused of passing forgeries and put in jail for two days—until my mother found out where he was and Uncle Federico came up with the cash to bail him out. Another time, they pulled over my uncle Julio while he was on his motorcycle. I was riding on the back. They demanded his license and threatened to seize his bike, accusing him of not wearing his helmet. He gave them fifty pesos, and they smirked and let us go. My uncle said it was hard for the policemen to survive on their low wages, so they needed kickbacks. But even at eleven, I knew it was horrible to lie, scam, and take bribes. If I were them, I would never rip off the poor working people I was supposed to protect. In stark contrast, I watched how professional and respectful the Americans in blue uniforms were, doing their jobs without expecting a payoff.

Yet the minute their squad cars drove away, there was more gun-fire. Did the robbers return to kill us so we wouldn't be able to identify who they were? Three loud pops came at us from the park across the street. The shots barely missed Mom, but our neighbor standing beside her shouted in pain. He held up his right arm, hit by a bullet. Someone tied a scarf around it to stop the blood. Another ambulance whisked him off to the same emergency room where they'd taken my father. We took shelter inside the building, locking all the doors and windows. I'd never been shot at or heard what a gun sounded like up close. There was nothing I could do. I was too small and helpless to save my family. It was the worst feeling in the world.

Uncle Federico pulled up in his cab to take Mom to Brookdale Hospital. "Go to your aunt Victoria's," he told me and my brother. "Stay there until we know more about your *papi*."

The police returned. They positioned themselves in front of our building all night to fend off other criminals. It calmed me to see they were there, but I wished they'd been patrolling the area sooner so two people wouldn't have been hurt. I almost lost both of my parents on the same day.

I later learned that my father had just parked his cab after a long shift when two guys surrounded him on both sides. He was carrying his taxi radio inside a backpack for safekeeping. They'd jumped him to steal the backpack and $170 in cash, all that he'd earned in sixteen hours of driving. It was a lot of money for us.

Two weeks earlier, when I first saw kids playing soccer on the sidewalk outside our seven-story gray walk-up with a fire escape, the neighborhood and the building seemed solid, a place we'd be safe. Not flimsy, like the roof of our wooden house back on my grandfather's farm that blew away during Hurricane David in 1979. I'd almost died as a newborn, according to my grandparents. That house also flooded when it rained. Our one-bedroom unit in New York was small, with a pullout couch instead of a bed I had to share with my brother, yet I felt sure this new brick home in a cluster of apartments, overstuffed with low-income families like ours, could withstand bad weather.

So far, the transition had been rough.

The pipes jangled at all hours. Reggae and hip-hop blasted from open windows and competed with the romantic songs of Ana Gabriel, a Mexican singer with a raspy voice, that Mom played as she cooked and cleaned. People hollered in tongues I didn't recognize. Car alarms blared all night from break-ins. Frames of vehicles on top of cinder-blocks with no doors, tires, or headlights lined abandoned streets, filled with litter and graffiti. You couldn't walk outside in the dark without a *ladrón* or gang member threatening you. More horrifying were the Telemundo reports of eighty-five taxi drivers in the boroughs getting murdered for their money or radios in the last year.

Even before I heard about the wave of crimes against cabbies, I was already afraid of this strange country. Crown Heights was nothing like the New York I'd seen in movies. Where were the fancy cars, skyscrapers, and fun crowds gathering in Times Square to watch the ball drop on New Year's Eve?

Since my parents had split when I was born, until we'd moved to Brooklyn I didn't know Dad at all. I'd never even seen his picture. I'd grown up with Mom, my older brother Tony, my grandparents, and my two other younger half siblings who had different dads. The first time I remembered meeting my father in person, I was nine. He visited our home in Villa Sinda, bringing silver BMX bikes for me and Tony. Those bikes were like a miracle. We didn't have anything like them on the farm where we played with rocks, pretending they were toys. We'd make baseballs out of old socks, cut finger holes in a piece of cardboard for a glove, use a stick as a bat and ashes from the firepit as bases.

After I thanked him, Mami told me, "Ask for a *bendición*," our daily custom.

"Bless me, Uncle," I complied, hiding behind her.

Mom laughed gently. "That's not your uncle, silly, that's your father."

Three years later, he was visiting again from the United States, staying with his parents, Grandpa Fillo and Grandma Andrea. It confused me. Where had he been my whole life? The next day Dad presented Tony and me with T-shirts, pants, dress shoes, and a cool battery-operated echo keychain that made the sound of a jetfighter, police siren, and bursts of gunfire. Mom sat us down. They were back together, she announced. We were moving to New York, where Dad had lived since 1983. He was a legal resident there, and a lawyer was helping him bring us over. I didn't like that we'd have to leave my half brother and half sister in the Dominican Republic, but Mom was so happy and hopeful, I tried to be too.

These last two weeks in the United States were the only time my family of four had ever slept under the same roof. Dad chaperoned me to my first day of school, to the doctor, and to get my first winter coat at the Pitkin Avenue Bargain Center. He showed me how to purchase train and bus tokens and bought me a map, instructing me in Spanish. In the States for more than a decade, he still didn't speak English well, though he understood everything. "Take this bus. The fare is fifty cents. Get off at the sixth stop. You pull the string when you want to get off."

After that, I was on my own.

I didn't want to be alone again. Dad couldn't afford to fly all of us to JFK at the same time, so Tony and Mom had gone first. I cried almost every night for a month at Grandma's, thinking I'd been abandoned. Since we didn't have a phone and long-distance calls from elsewhere were too expensive to make, I wrote letters to my father, pleading with him not to forget me. I was pumped when Grandma said he'd borrowed enough cash for my fare a month later; my begging had worked.

I was up for my flight at four in the morning. It was my first time on a plane. I imagined putting my hand out to touch the clouds, but the windows wouldn't open. I was so excited to fly with Evelina, a family friend who held my hand and got me Coca-Cola and peanuts and then dinner of mashed potatoes, beef, and rice. The stewardess gave me a little plastic red, white, and blue plane with the American Airlines logo. I treasured that toy for a long time, taking it as a sign of good things to come. In my homeland, I'd slept on a mattress with my brother, cousin, and Uncle Carlos, eating mostly what we'd grown and picked ourselves in the fields. I had just a few shirts and pants. We hardly had running water or electricity. In the United States, I pictured getting my own room in a bigger home with lots of clothes, different food, fun toys, and a big color TV. That wasn't how things panned out.

I got used to living in our new cramped place, playing tag and hide and seek with my cousins. One day, I turned to Modesto and asked, "Who are those guys wearing long black coats and hats?"

"They're religious Jews," he explained. "They're angry at some Black neighbors who started fires and looted their stores after a car accident killed a kid."

A reporter on Spanish TV said that Crown Heights had been the site of a riot the previous summer. Racial tensions persisted. On my way to school my first week, I found myself in the middle of protests.

Seeing how violent Eastern Parkway was, I wished we could go back home. We might have been poor farm workers, bouncing between both grandparents depending on when they needed help planting tobacco and corn crops, but at least—except for storms—we'd felt safe there.

Everything was harder here. In the mornings Dad went to work at 5:00 a.m. He didn't get home until 9:00 p.m. When I did see him, I wanted to tell him about my math class and debate the stats of Dominican ball players like Sammy Sosa and Pedro Martínez. But he didn't care about school or sports. He was too tired from working to play with me. Instead, I'd say goodnight and "*Cíon papi querido,*" asking for another blessing. He'd reply "*Dios te bendiga,*" God bless you. I wished I could hug or kiss him or have him tuck me in, but we didn't have that kind of relationship.

Wasn't life supposed to be easier in America? I missed my grandparents. But even if Dad wanted to, he couldn't afford return tickets to the DR. He could barely cover the bills. He was very frugal, insisting he made only enough for our rent and meals and to send money to his relatives 1,500 miles away. That was why Mom cooked big batches of Dominican-style beef and chicken *pastelitos*. She went store to store, selling them for a dollar each to get us more food and school supplies, sending anything extra to her kin. After class, I delivered her orders. My clothes always smelled like fried dough, which made me feel poor.

Any mention of money made my parents argue louder.

"*Hija de la semilla!* Son of a bitch, the whole place reeks of your chicken *pastelitos,*" Dad complained.

Mom would open the windows and close the bedroom door behind him, putting towels underneath to block out the smell. But then the whole apartment would be freezing.

It hurt my ears when he spoke to her so harshly.

"It's nothing," she'd say, though it made me worry he'd disappear again and leave us to fend for ourselves in this dangerous new city.

The night of Dad's stabbing, Tony and I slept at Aunt Victoria's, on the other side of the building, with her three kids. The next morning, my parents were still at the hospital. Tía Victoria sent us to school, not knowing if Dad had survived. After finishing his homework, Tony played *Super Mario Bros.* and *Street Fighter II* with the other boys. I couldn't get into it. I prayed my father wouldn't die, so I'd have a chance to know him. Cousin Benny handed me his Derek Jeter and Sammy Sosa baseball cards. "I want you to have these," he said, putting his arm around me.

"Thank you," I told him, touched. "But that's okay. You don't have to give me anything."

"They're yours. They'll make you feel better," he insisted, promising we could get plastic sleeves at the store to protect them.

"*Quilo, no te preocupe,*" my aunt reassured me. "Don't worry, everything will be okay."

I knew it wouldn't.

After school on Tuesday, Mom still hadn't come home. Finally, we were told to clean up and Uncle Federico drove us in his cab to join Mom at Brookdale. The hospital was cold and only Mom could go in; Tony and I had to wait until visiting hours. My father was in bed, wearing a blue hospital gown, attached to a machine with flashing lights they called a heart monitor. I was afraid the sliding doors to Dad's room would close on me, so I stayed outside.

He'd been stabbed several times in his arm and had lost a lot of blood, Mom told us. She looked exhausted. The doctor explained that Dad was sedated and in and out of consciousness. When I asked what that meant, he told us Dad would be sleepy and couldn't talk much. I was relieved when my father eyed me and nodded. I went over and hugged him carefully so I wouldn't hurt him. He reached for my hand and squeezed it, as if to say, "I'm glad you're here, son, I love you," but as usual he didn't have the words.

The next time I visited he was more alert, grateful to be alive, but worrying about our lack of cash and health insurance. "I'm sorry I can't work now. We owe the landlord. I hope you guys can pick up the slack," he said to me and Tony. "Keep making those *pastelitos,*" he told Mom.

"Oh, now you like them?" she asked.

He was on an IV drip and the nurse mentioned the blood type he needed. I wished I could give him mine, but Mom said twelve was too young to donate. He was in stable condition, the doctor told us, but still fragile.

We all were, for years.

2

Secretos y Mentiras

Brooklyn, March 1994

As Dad recovered, life was looking up. We settled into a comfortable rhythm. After school, Tony and I played baseball in the park. Mom worked as a chef at a local eatery, and she often brought home rotisserie chicken with oregano, rice, peas, and pepper, with delicious flan for dessert. With Dad not driving his cab, he was around to share meals more often. It felt like we were becoming a normal family at last.

By age sixteen, Tony had taken a job as a mechanic on evenings and weekends. While I kept delivering Mom's fried Dominican sandwiches each afternoon, at fourteen I started stocking shelves for the bodega a block away. The shop was owned by Dominican immigrants who admired how fast I unloaded boxes from trucks and gave me $100 a week in cash. I felt flush.

"Always share what you have with your relatives and help out the less fortunate," Grandpa Fillo taught me. Our priest pushed us to give

10 percent to the church. I liked doing my part, and only *kept* 10 percent of my salary, giving the rest to my grandparents in the Caribbean and to Mom.

I looked forward to *Noche Buena*, Christmas Eve, especially the roast pork, mixed rice, pigeon peas, potato salad, and guava cake. To make the holidays special for my family, I drew cards with magic markers and used my bodega salary to buy gifts: a Yankees hat for Tony, a beige blouse for Mom, and a blue sweater for Dad. He thanked me and gave me a hug. As he showed me and Tony the holiday lights in Brooklyn and Queens, we had a chance to get to know him better. Still, I never knew what would set him off.

"You're spending too much on crap," Dad told me one morning, staring at my new white and red Nikes and blue JanSport backpack.

I usually stayed quiet when he made angry accusations. But today I defended myself. "All the kids at school have them, Papi. I really wanted them."

"Where's the receipt?" he said. "You should have asked me first."

"But I worked to save for it myself," I blurted out.

"He's a good boy, Jose," Mom told Dad as I gave her my salary. "Thanks for pitching in, Quilo." She kissed my forehead, handing me back a few bucks so I could get whatever else I wanted.

Tony landed me a part-time gig at the auto repair shop. We kept clocking in hours and saving, buying new bicycles to get to work. We never missed a shift, even when there was two feet of snow on the ground and our hands were frozen. We'd fall, then get up and keep riding, the only kids on bikes in the winter storm.

Back home, I'd earned Bs, but two years after landing in America, school remained complicated. I butchered the language, and still thought and dreamt in Spanish. My folks just used our native tongue and watched only Telemundo on TV. At Mahalia Jackson Junior High, I was put in the ESL class. Taking an assessment test in the English I couldn't understand, I filled in boxes in a zigzag pattern on the answer sheet and flunked. I didn't tell my folks. They never mentioned my low grades. My homeroom teacher ignored me every time I raised my hand. Frustrated, I asked a bilingual classmate to translate. Rather than find some way to help me, the teacher scolded me, sending me to the principal's office for "disrupting the class." I was failing everything but Spanish and physical education. I was good at baseball. Still, I felt dumb and depressed, so I focused on other things. I took a higher-paying job at a car wash, which pleased Mom. Then romance hit. In homeroom, a pretty Dominican girl with long curly dark hair sat next to me. Mariela was a straight-A student. When she came over to sit with me in the cafeteria, I knew she liked me too. I gave her my chocolate chip cookie and M&M's and wrote poetry and made drawings to impress her.

"Look at the lovebirds," my classmates teased.

One day, Tony and I came home from work to screaming. Walking in the door, we heard Dad yell, "Here's the fucking money," and saw him throw ten singles on the floor, then march into the bedroom and slam the door.

Crying, Mom explained that after she'd paid all their bills with what she earned herself, she only had enough to buy rice and beans for dinner. So she asked him for ten dollars to get chicken wings at the nearby Chinese restaurant.

"Don't worry about it," I said, feeling bad Dad was being such a jerk. I dug into my pocket and pulled out five singles I'd been given as tips at my job and handed them to her.

"He can keep his damn money," Tony added, handing her a fiver.

She nodded, thanking us. "Quilo, want to come with me to get the food?"

"Sure," I said. On the way, I asked her if she knew the words for "chicken wings" in English or Chinese.

"I just do this," she said, putting her hands under her arms and flapping.

"Are you kidding me?" I asked.

She wasn't and we both cracked up. Sure enough, at the restaurant, since they spoke only Chinese, she made the flapping gesture, held up ten fingers and they prepared $10 worth of wings for her.

At home, I noticed my father had taken the singles off the floor and put them next to his wallet. After he saw Mom put the bag on the counter, he reached in and took three wings for himself, shoving them into his mouth, quickly eating the food he didn't pay for. It upset me.

A week later, on the way home from school, I was daydreaming about asking Mariela to be my girlfriend when Mom threw open the door, hysterical. "*Es tu padre*," she cried.

My father had been attacked a second time, worse than before. A fare he'd picked up reached over from the back seat to stab him with a kitchen knife in the right side of his stomach, she told me, then he stole all of his money. Several organs were punctured. Life or death.

Uncle Federico rushed over to get us in his cab. I asked about the plastic barrier separating the front and back seats. He said it was to prevent robberies, showing me how it worked.

"Didn't Papi have one too in his taxi?" I wanted to know, feeling sick in the gut.

"Yes. But he must have forgotten to raise it." He shook his head and hit the steering wheel, swearing. "*Coño maldita sea*."

At the same hospital as before, Dad was connected to different machines and this time he seemed almost dead. Wearing a green gown, he was hooked up to a heart monitor, with a tube inside his mouth and an IV in his arm. With his eyes closed and gray stubble on his chin from not shaving, he seemed older. He hardly looked alive. They gave Mom a plastic bag with his watch and ring. The doctor said he was in a coma and if he didn't respond soon, they'd have to take him off life support. For several days, I held his hand and squeezed it, hoping he'd respond. Regardless of how he treated us, he was still my dad. I didn't want him to die.

Luckily, that week he slowly woke up. But one afternoon when

Mom and I walked into his room for a visit, a lady was already there, leaning over his bed, whispering and holding his hand. She was all dolled up, with big blond hair, heels, red lipstick, and perfume. Although my mother wore jeans, sneakers, and a ponytail with no makeup, she was prettier than the woman. But rushing between work, making *pastelitos*, and visiting Dad in the hospital didn't leave her much time to be glamourous. The fancy blond lady stared intently at my mother, looking her up and down.

"You got five minutes to leave, lady. When I get back, you better be gone," Mom hissed, her lip twitching, like she was about to break down. "I'm going for a walk." She left me standing there.

The blond woman hugged Dad quickly and said, "We'll talk later."

"She's just my friend," Dad told me when she left.

Oblivious to what I had just witnessed, I felt whiplashed and wasn't sure who to worry about more—my father lying there almost dead or my mother freaking out, escaping so I wouldn't see her cry.

"*Quién era ella?*" Mom demanded when she got back.

"Estela heard I was dying and got emotional," he tried to explain.

He kept assuring us that this "Estela" was just "a friend" from his past. I chose to believe him until the Friday afternoon a month later when he was discharged. He needed to rest well at home, his nurse explained. I quickly moved all the furniture around in my parents' bedroom to make him comfortable, so he wouldn't have to get up. I bought him a longer phone cord and set his landline up on a table close by so he could call our relatives. Stuff on his nightstand fell. Picking it up, I noticed a bunch of pictures in an envelope. I scanned for a shot of myself in the stack. Instead, I saw a photo of two kids—a boy and girl—I didn't recognize, maybe three and four years old. The boy looked like me at that age.

"Who are they?" I asked him.

"They're your cousins," he said.

I ran through all my uncles and aunts' children in my mind, as well as the relatives from my mother's side. "From where? Who are their parents?"

"Don't worry about it," he mumbled.

Something was off. Why would he have photos of cousins I'd never seen? If they were from his family, wouldn't I know them? They'd be related to me too.

In the following weeks, the phone rang at all hours. I'd pick up, but the caller kept hanging up. One night, Mom answered. I heard Estela yell through the receiver, "He's mine, he still wants to be with me." Mom was fuming.

It took me a while to figure it all out: Dad had lived with Estela during the years my folks were separated. After they broke up, he came back to us. The "cousins" Dad told me about were actually my half siblings. I couldn't believe my father had two children with Estela that he never told us about. They lived in New York too, nearby. I could have walked by my own sister and brother on the street without knowing it. My mother had also had two kids with someone else after they split— my younger brother Giovanny and little sister Liliana. They lived with their grandparents in the Dominican Republic. We kept in touch using phone cards and sent letters overseas every week. The difference was Mom never lied or hid the truth from us or Dad.

My mother felt shell-shocked and betrayed, like I did. She continued to feed, clean, and take care of my father, but she was quieter. They barely spoke.

So that was the real reason Dad was always coming home so late and money was so tight that he could barely afford to pay for chicken wings: he had to earn enough for two families! The way he spent his salary was his business, but it wasn't right for him to take the cash I worked hard for. It wasn't my job to help support the second household he'd lied about. From then on, I did what I wanted with my money.

I pictured telling my girl Mariela everything horrible that happened, but at our homeroom Monday morning, she was missing. I was told that she'd moved away. A friend of hers gave me her phone and beeper number. I tried both over and over. She never answered. No matter who I asked, I couldn't find her whereabouts. Mariela didn't even say goodbye.

Everything around me felt like it was spinning. I wanted to escape. I warned my mother that I was saving up enough to fly back to my beloved Grandpa Fillo's farm in the Dominican Republic, where I belonged. I didn't want to stay in a country that didn't want me, with bad guys who kept knifing my father and a woman with two more kids trying to steal him away, just when I'd finally found him. The whole world seemed unfair and broken and I couldn't fix it.

3

There's Nothing for You Here

The Dominican Republic, December 1995

FAILING FIVE OUT OF SEVEN CLASSES IN NINTH GRADE, I felt lost and depressed, so I cut school to play hoops on the street. One day, reaching out for the basketball, a teammate elbowed me in the head. Dizzy, I dropped to the ground, dripping blood. I grabbed a shirt and pressed it to the wound to stop the bleeding as I rushed two blocks to the nearby Kings County Hospital emergency room. I gave a false name since we had no insurance. I needed four stitches above my right eye. I brushed my long, curly hair in front to hide the scar from my parents, dreading their disappointment, sure they'd punish me. But they had too many problems to notice my wound, my bad marks, or my delinquency. Dad hadn't recovered from his second stabbing. Mom was exhausted from working so hard to make up for the salary he was losing. She barely spoke to him after discovering his other family. Not wanting to add to their burdens, I didn't mention how badly school was going, forged their signature on my report card, and hatched a secret plan. I picked up hours at the car wash and the tire shop every afternoon and weekend. I made $60 a day plus tips and managed to save $2,000, enough to move home to the island.

"I don't want to be here anymore," I told Mom. "I'm better off back on Grandpa's farm."

"What's wrong, Quilo?" she asked, alarmed. "You can tell me anything."

What wasn't wrong? "Learning English is too hard. Nobody helps me. When I can't say the words right, kids at school laugh at me. I asked Mrs. Wilson, but she sends me to the principal's office for detentions," I blurted out, choking up. "I flunked most of my classes. I can't do it anymore."

"Ay Quilo, I'm sorry," she said, looking shocked. "Come, give me a hug." She wiped away my tears, then held me.

I missed farm life, animals, fresh air, climbing trees. I was lonely here, even working with my brother at the tire shop. It freaked me out when Tony got detained and almost arrested for defending himself in a fight. After some kids tried to steal my new bookbag, I was constantly petrified I'd get jumped by a gang or stabbed like Dad. I didn't even tell her how horrifying it was to see him in a coma and then find out he was a liar with another wife and two kids, or that Mariela had disappeared without saying goodbye.

I held Mom tight. "I just don't fit in here. Dad's always weird and angry. Tony's older and doesn't want to hang out with me. I miss Grandpa Fillo, Giovanny, and Liliana." I'd shared photos and stories about the bridges and skyscrapers in America with my relatives back home, but since the mail took so long and often got lost, it was easier to wait for someone from the DR to take them on the plane and bring us their responses to Brooklyn. "I hate waiting a month to get their letters."

"I was so worried about money and your father, I didn't see you were hurting," Mom said.

"I can cover the plane ticket home. I already packed." I pretended I just wanted to go for a vacation. She didn't know I planned to stay.

"I don't want you flying alone," Mom replied. I thought she would tell me I couldn't go, but she surprised me by saying, "I'll go with you when I have enough to pay for my own ticket."

"Really?" I asked. "I'll work harder to help you. Let's sell more beef *pastelitos*."

Dad had healed enough to drive his cab again and Mom added hours to her two jobs. We saved the money quickly. I brought $600 cash to a nearby travel agency where the owner agreed to make the reservation for me. She handed me the tickets the next afternoon. I was so excited I didn't mind paying for two round trips, even though I wouldn't be taking the return flight in a month. We would be flying out in early December, just me and Mom. Tony didn't want to come with us—he planned to go on his own over the summer. I hadn't seen my relatives in three whole years. I couldn't wait to move back.

I hustled even harder to make extra bucks for Christmas presents. At the inexpensive Chinese bazaar on Utica Avenue, I bought gifts for my relatives. I filled a suitcase with Nike sneakers, Hugo Boss T-shirts, underwear, a Nintendo Game Boy for Giovanny and Liliana, a $15 flowery dress for Grandma Andrea, $10 dress pants for Grandpa Bienvenido, and a jacket and matching slacks for Grandpa Fillo. On the pant leg, I noticed a label, "Made in the Dominican Republic," probably where one of my kin worked at a sweatshop. It felt nuts that they were making clothes they couldn't afford to buy, and I was bringing them pants they'd probably sewn for themselves.

For my aunts, uncles, and cousins I found miniature soaps, shampoos, and toothpaste—much cheaper in America. Mom picked out perfume for her mother, but I had a special treat for Grandma Josefita: M&M's, Skittles, and jelly beans. When I was seven, she'd sent me to the store with a note to buy sugar and cinnamon, saying, "Keep the change." I spent the extra on candy I chomped on the way home.

When she asked me for a piece, I put the last one in my mouth and said, "Only if you give me more money."

"I just gave you money and you won't share with me?" she laughed. It became our joke.

Dad saw us pack but only told me, "Give this $130 to Grandma Andrea." He didn't say anything to Mom. Their relationship had deteriorated since we'd caught him at the hospital with Estela, who had the nerve to keep calling to accuse Mom of taking her man and stealing her kids' father. When my parents did speak, they argued. I wondered if he wanted us out of the way so he could be with her and *their* kids.

To make everything worse, without asking Mom, Dad let his newly arrived thirty-year-old cousin Agusto move in with us "temporarily." I liked Agusto. Back home, he was a bus driver who used to give me free rides between my grandparents' farms. But him living with us meant that Tony and I had to sleep together with Agusto on the pullout. So I was cramped and uncomfortable in my own bed every night. I wasn't surprised that my father didn't offer to take us to the airport or pay the cab fare. Instead, I asked Uncle Federico, Dad's brother, to drive us to JFK at 8:00 a.m. I was nervous the flight would get canceled since it was snowing outside, but it wasn't even delayed.

Wanting to go home looking like a winner, I wore my Scottie Pippen Nike sneakers, new Tommy Hilfiger beige pants, and blue Hugo Boss jacket. We checked four bags and a carry-on, plus my backpack stuffed with gifts. Almost everyone on the plane spoke Spanish and, like us, carried gifts for their *familias*. I ate the *moro de abichuela y pollo*, the mixed chicken, rice, and beans dinner they served, and drank my fill of free Cokes and orange juice. In the middle of the three-and-a-half-hour flight, there was a lot of turbulence. The flight attendant told everyone to put away their drinks and cigarettes and put up their seats. Mom's face went white. I held her hand, wondering how to tell her I wasn't accompanying her back to America.

When we landed, all the passengers clapped. They made the sign of the cross and kissed their thumbs, saying, *"Gracias a Dios."* I was pumped walking through the crowded, chaotic airport. Dominican singers played merengue *ripiao* with an accordion, tambura, guitar, *trumpeta*, and *güira*, welcoming me home. Everyone resembled and spoke like me. For the first time in three years, I was where I belonged, with my people.

"Let's exchange money here," I told Mom, following the signs. We changed $200 for pesos. At the baggage claim, we found our bags, then stood in a disorganized zigzag line at customs. It was a mess and took more than an hour. Everything was checked by hand instead of by X-ray like in America. The workers haphazardly lifted clothes from our luggage, rifling through our stuff for "contraband."

"Where are the black sneakers for Uncle Carlos?" Mom asked as we closed the bags up.

"I don't see them," I said.

She shook her head and whispered, "The customs guy stole them, I knew I should keep my eyes on him." In Brooklyn we might have yelled for the police if someone blatantly ripped us off. Here, there was nothing we could do since, I remembered, you never knew which cops were corrupt and would push for a bribe. At least they didn't take Grandma's M&M's.

During the exit inspection, the customs guy broke the zipper on Mom's luggage, so I wrapped the bag with my shoelaces and a belt. Carrying my backpack, I toted the mended suitcase on my shoulder and pushed a cart with our other four bags in front of me. I was sweating in the coat I no longer needed, but I was so glad I'd escaped cold, dirty, slushy New York. Outside, the warm, sunny 80 degrees kissed my skin. People held up signs with names. I looked for Uncle Carlos, Mom's brother. At eighteen, he was older than me. He saw us and waved.

"Quilo, Sabina!" he called, hugging us hello. I was pleased he was wearing the short sleeve shirt and Levi's jeans we'd sent him. "This is my girlfriend, Yoenia." She nodded hi as he pointed to where he was parked. A porter rushed in front of me and cleared the path for us.

"*Hermano*, aren't you going to give me money for helping you?" he asked.

"Helping me with what? I'm not your brother and I carried all the bags by myself," I said. I couldn't believe this clown wanted a tip for doing nothing. I'd forgotten you had to watch out for guys on the take here and the only people you could trust were your family.

"Please? Something for Christmas?" he begged.

I gave him the quarters I had in my pocket. "Maybe he needs it for a kid?" I told Mom as Uncle Carlos shrugged.

He and Yoenia helped us stuff everything inside the car. It was an hour and a half ride to my grandfather's farm. I enjoyed staring at the palm trees and grass and watching the ridge lines of mountains I'd dreamt of. I hung my head out the window and felt the Caribbean breeze on my face. Passing vending stands on the streets made me feel starved. We stopped to buy fried fish and pink guavas that I devoured right away. They tasted better than anything I'd eaten in Crown Heights.

After blowing the car's horn to announce ourselves, we were greeted by Grandma Josefita, grayer than I remembered, and Grandpa Bienvenido, with more wrinkles under his eyes. A dozen relatives hugged me and Mom, saying "*Cuánto tiempo*," long time. I was touched by the reception. It felt nice to be back at my grandparents' five-bedroom house, which sat on an acre of land. It had electricity but no running water. We used an outside latrine. To compensate for the last drought, Grandpa was working as a butcher at a slaughterhouse in case the crops didn't pay off.

"How are you? We missed you," my cousins said, taking our bags to the bedroom. After greeting everyone, I opened my luggage and quickly gave out all the presents, feeling older, rich, and generous, like Santa Claus.

My eleven-year-old half brother Giovanny was so happy with the Chicago Bulls T-shirt and Nike sneakers that he put them right on. Liliana played the Nintendo Game Boy on the spot. Grandma opened her bag of candy, cracked up, and kissed my forehead.

"When he was younger, he wouldn't give me any of his candy," she said, though everybody already knew the story. "Now he shares with me."

When I'd lived here, loved ones returning from abroad would be honored with big feasts. Now we were the ones being feted, like foreign dignitaries. They'd prepared a goat—sun-dried and seasoned with lemon, salt, and oregano—for a big dinner with a tomato salad, cabbage, and *arroz gandules*, my favorite side dish of rice and peas.

"What's it like in Brooklyn?" everyone asked during dinner. I showed off pictures of New York I'd taken with a disposable Kodak camera.

More questions followed: Is it hard to learn English? How's school? How's the food? How's work? How much money do you make? Is it easy to get rich there?

"No," I answered. "You have to work a lot and hard. Rent and food are very expensive."

I made small talk, feeling important, acting like everything in the U.S. was wonderful. I was not ready to announce that I was staying. First, I had to break it to my mother.

In the past, I'd shared a bedroom here with a cousin, Giovanny, and my uncle. On this visit my grandparents gave me my own room. In the morning, they served me a traditional Dominican breakfast of *mangú*: eggs with thick salami, cheese, onions, smashed green plantain, and butter—so much better than the Cheerios we had in Crown Heights. All I had to do to be treated like a prince was move away!

The next day I hired a family friend to drive me an hour by motorcycle on an unpaved, bumpy, dusty road to Dad's parents' farm in Los Limones. Their house was smaller, with no electricity, but had more acres for farming. I loved being the guest of honor at another feast: roast pork and potato salad, with ten relatives from that side of the family. I gave out the shampoos, toothpastes, toiletries, and toys, and a dress for Grandma Andrea. She looked a little heavier as she kissed me, suddenly more affectionate. To Grandpa Fillo, my favorite, I gave pants, a shirt, and a black tie. That night, instead of putting a pillow over my head to muffle sirens, gun shots, and rap music blasting, I drifted off to sleep to the sounds of crickets and chirping birds. Even waking up to the rooster crowing at 5:00 a.m., I slept more soundly than I had in three years. Hearing Grandpa get up early, I put on clothes to join him for his daily chores.

We fed his animals. I saddled his donkey and ran with Collar, his dog. It was drizzling outside, and I started coughing. I used to get sick working on his farm every morning. A doctor said I had asthma, but the medicine he prescribed was too expensive and didn't work well, so Mom took me to a healer who gave me castor oil with ground cotton seed and said a prayer and it mostly went away.

As the sun came out, we took a walk to the fields where I'd worked with him. I climbed a tree like I used to, picking *quenepas*, guavas, and mangos, eating a few quickly, savoring the sweet and sour mix.

"So what's up, Quilo? You okay?"

"I'm okay, Grandpa."

"How are you really doing?" he asked, looking into my eyes.

I sat on a boulder as Grandpa and Collar followed me. "Honestly, I don't like it there. I miss you," I confessed. I told him all the crazy shit that happened: Dad's two stabbings, my folks' horrible fights, butchering the language, my bad grades, getting detentions for nothing, how I felt like an outcast. "I want to stay here with you," I added. "I'll help you on the farm."

"We miss you too, Quilo," he said. "But it's very hard here. I wake up to work before dawn and go to sleep exhausted, seven days a week. I'm always tired, no time off. Things are getting harder. If it's not a hurricane, it's a drought where we have to feed the animals and water the crops by hand. I had to sell my cattle so they didn't starve because it hardly rains. The lagoons have dried up too."

"So you could use me here," I said. "And luckily, you still have all your own land."

"You're the lucky one to be in *los Estados Unidos*," he said. "You know, it took your dad years to get the documents and money for your immigration visa. Lots of people we know got denied."

I'd heard of family friends desperate to get over to the United States who'd had no luck finding a sponsor. I never thought of what my father had to go through to bring me, Mom, and Tony over. My cousin told me there were only two ways out of poverty here—move to America or get signed to a baseball team in the DR. Unfortunately, I wasn't a good enough athlete.

"You can make a much better life for yourself over there," Grandpa said. "You can go further than me and your parents and become more than we could."

"I don't have a better life," I snapped. "It's way worse."

"You're having a rough time now in classes because of the language barrier. And you have us here to fall back on. But don't give up yet. I never even got the chance to go to school," he said. "My parents needed me to work the farm. I never learned to read or write. I always regretted that, to this day. After we married, your grandma had to teach me how to sign my name. Your father couldn't finish high school either."

"I can't read or write English or communicate with anyone there," I complained. "People make fun of me."

"After you learn the language, it will be much easier."

"I can't do it. It's impossible!" I raised my voice. He wasn't getting it.

"Aren't there any teachers there who speak Spanish? Ask one for extra help," he suggested. "Please try a little harder, Quilo. Find a solution. Do it for me."

Working in the field again, I remembered how exhausting farming was, how run-down I used to get, how burdened I'd felt by the responsibility of having to walk hours to feed the horses and cows twice a day. Tony and I milked them and picked the beans and tobacco crops each morning in the hot sun and sometimes when it was pouring outside. If we didn't finish or the lousy weather slowed us down, we had to miss school, sometimes for a whole week. We never had fun with friends. Once, after we played in the lagoon and didn't feed Grandpa Bienvenido's donkey when he wanted, he hit me and Tony with a wet lasso. He whipped Tony so hard on his stomach that his belly button got all swollen. Tony cursed and threw rocks at him, then left to live with Grandfather Fillo. But Fillo could be a tough taskmaster too, if we didn't do what he said immediately. I'd forgotten how difficult it was here.

"*Te amo*, Quilo. Don't give up yet. Things will brighten up. You're a good boy. You're going to have a great future there," he promised.

As I gave him a hug, he patted my head. I missed being with him. He was the father figure I trusted most. My dad never hugged me or told me I was good.

Late that evening, I asked Grandma Andrea, "Why isn't Grandpa back yet?"

"He had to fix the fence. Some thieves were stealing his harvest," she said.

"How's he doing lately?" I wanted her take.

"Not so good. He hardly sleeps. He gets up too early and comes back when it's dark out. He's only fifty but constantly in pain, with muscle aches and cramps. He misses doctors' appointments," she said. "I have to send someone to bring him food or he won't eat because he has too many chores to do. I worry about him. He has enemies who cut his trees and steal his harvest. He comes home so late with no flashlight or lamp."

The second week of January, right before we were supposed to leave for New York, I hugged Grandpa Fillo for a long time, sure I could talk him into letting me stay.

"I don't want to go," I told him, clinging, holding back tears. "You need help on the farm. I want to live here and work with you."

"You have to go, Quilo. There's nothing for you here." He ruffled my hair. "Go do the things I never had a chance to. You'll come back to visit. But you need to make your life over there now."

I thought of what he told me, how sick he was of working the farm his whole life, how he regretted not learning to read and write. Maybe I should listen to him and give the United States another chance? Tony, Mom, Uncle Federico, and my new friends were in Brooklyn. So was Dad, who was ornery and unfaithful but never beat us. I reminded myself of the good things about America: we had electricity and indoor plumbing, and I never had to miss school to pick plantains or feed the donkey. There were cute girls I liked in my grade. Stocking shelves at the bodega paid better for a lot less hours than farming. America had more sports teams. But skipping school to hang out on the street and flunking my classes, I was wasting my chance. Grandpa was right. I should try to do better.

"Here, take this," Fillo said, handing me a tiny card with a picture of Saint Clara on it. "She'll watch over you." He added a small piece of paper he'd had Grandma write on, wrapped up in the shape of cross with clear tape and two staples. "And this is my prayer, only for you. For good luck."

Without reading either one, I put both in my wallet, where they stayed for decades, the note never opened but still making me feel like he was always there, protecting me.

4

By Heart

New York, January 1996

I PUT THE LIQUID DULCE DE LECHE, THE CARAMEL CANDY my grandparents made, on the table for Dad. He ate some but didn't thank me. I brought my brother the hard kind with shredded coconut that he liked.

"Thanks, Aquilino. How was your trip?" Tony asked.

"Good. I visited our baseball field, same dirt. I did a pickup game with town kids and went to the rooster fight. And I stayed with Grandpa Fillo a few days." I longed to tell Tony that I almost hadn't come back. But ever since he switched to a different public school, where he had a new girlfriend and best friend named Chino, we didn't confide much in each other anymore.

"The land is drier and Grandpa sold all of his cattle because of the drought. He just kept the horse, donkey, and dog. Otherwise, nothing changed," I said.

Nothing changed at school either. Nobody realized I'd missed three weeks. The only messages I had were from Bell Atlantic to pay the phone bills I'd put in my name. Nobody else cared. I was invisible. The freezing weather, with a snowstorm my first day back, didn't help my mood. I couldn't bear to face my father, the teachers who flunked me, and the language barrier I couldn't fix.

Sitting down for my first morning class, Gregory, a tall Honduran bully in my grade, looked at me and said, "Move. That's my seat."

"I'm already sitting here," I told him.

"Find another chair. Or you can suck my dick," he taunted.

I'd never heard that expression before and asked a Dominican classmate what it meant. When he explained, I jumped from my desk and clenched my fist, ready to explode and punch him.

Before blows were thrown, my new history instructor, Ms. Rodriguez, walked in and made us take our seats. She was tall and had graying hair like my grandmas, with kind brown eyes. After the period was over, she put her hand on my shoulder and stopped me from leaving. She asked, in Spanish, why I'd been out of school. Someone had noticed.

"I was visiting the Dominican Republic," I told her, comforted to hear a teacher speaking my native tongue.

"We thought you transferred. Or something bad happened to you. Do your parents know how many days you missed?" she asked. The way she spoke faster than me, pronouncing "R" as "L" and the "S" sound as an "H" like Rosie Perez in *Do the Right Thing*, I guessed she was from Puerto Rico.

"I was with my mom," I explained.

"But you're flunking out," Ms. Rodriguez said. "Why did she let you take a trip that would cause more absences?"

My mother had other things on her mind, I wanted to answer—like working two jobs because Dad almost died twice, then learning he had a whole other family. She was having a much worse time than

I was. I wondered if Mom had also wanted to move back to the DR. Was that why we stayed so long? Had she been ready to give up on Dad and America too?

"Are things okay at home?" Ms. Rodriguez said in a softer voice. She seemed to care.

I confessed I was having problems adjusting and couldn't master the new language. "It's horrible not understanding anything. I didn't even know the insult Gregory used." I quietly asked, "Can you help me?"

She nodded and told me to sign up for her social studies class. She let me make up the history final I'd missed and offered to tutor me after school, during lunch, or at recess. I committed to working with her every day for the year, reading books in English. We started right away. She opened our textbook and pointed to a page in the middle.

"This is how you pronounce *patriot*," she said. "You can do it. Focus. Say it again, until you get it right." She turned to the end, and we read: "I pledge allegiance to the Flag of the United States of America . . ."

"Keep repeating it," she instructed. "Until you know it by heart."

I wasn't clear on the difference between Social Studies I and II, U.S. History I and II, or Global History, but decided I would take all the courses I could that Ms. Rodriguez taught.

That same day, as my Spanish teacher took attendance, I heard her call out "Isabel Navarro." Recognizing the last name, I turned to see an adorable girl wearing hip black baggy pants, sneakers, and a blue jean jacket who had long hair with bangs. I tried not to stare at the little scar on her upper lip.

"Do you know Martin and Ivan Navarro?" I asked her on the way out of class, hoping she was related to the Dominican boys I'd recently played basketball with.

"They're my brothers," she said. "I have three. Two go here. Miguel's in middle school."

"I know them! They're cool. They didn't tell me they had such a pretty sister." It was the most boldly I'd ever flirted.

She smiled, not even embarrassed, as we turned left toward math. "Hey, are you following me?" I teased. Isabel said she was also going to Mr. Diaz's algebra class. "For real? Let me see," I asked. Comparing printouts, I was psyched we had almost the same schedule. "So you are stalking me."

"You wish," she said. I did!

After school I asked if I could carry her books home. She handed them over. "Want to study together since you speak English better and you're smarter?" I asked on the way.

"You know it, boy," she laughed, asking for my phone number.

I liked that she wasn't shy. She was sarcastic, with a playful sense of humor. When we reached her place, she gave me a peck on the cheek. She wasn't my first kiss, but I was falling for my first love. I took the B12 bus a few miles back to my place. The next afternoon, she said, "I think my mom saw us on the street yesterday," like that was a bad thing.

"What's wrong with her knowing we like each other?" I asked, worried she might not be allowed to have a boyfriend.

"She asked who you were, where you live, if you come from a good family," Isabel said.

"If you have me over, I'll answer all those questions myself," I replied.

She promptly invited me to study at her place and meet her parents. Their apartment was bigger than mine. Her brothers slept on bunk beds in one room, but she had her own bedroom. They asked me to stay for a dinner of rice, beans, salad, and beef stew, similar to what Mom made. Everyone spoke Spanish, like our home. Her father asked where we were from in the DR and it turned out their hometown was only a half hour from Villa Sinda.

"What does your father do for work?" he asked.

"He's a taxi driver, sir," I said. "And I've worked at S&G Tire Shop for the past year and a half, after school and on weekends." To clear up any concerns he might have about my reputation, I reassured him I was the clean-cut, hard-working type, in case her brothers hadn't already vouched for me. Nervous, I wondered whether Isabel had brought other guys home before. If so, I wanted him to like me more.

"What do you do at the tire shop?" he asked, mentioning that Isabel's two older brothers all worked part-time at an auto parts warehouse with him.

"I'm selling and mounting new and used tires, changing flats, fixing breaks, and helping the boss set up the vehicles for wheel alignment, sir."

Since he was in the car business, he was interested in the details. Or maybe he was trying to figure out what I would do with my life, if I was an honest guy who'd make something of himself and be a respectable husband for his only daughter. Afterward, Martin turned on the radio to a bachata song by Luis Vargas. They reminded me of my family, only normal and happy.

"I should get home now," I told Isabel's parents. "It was a pleasure to meet you."

She waited with me by the window, holding my hand, until we saw the bus come down her street.

That Friday, Ms. Vega, the guidance counselor, stopped me in the hallway to tell me to come to her office. I guessed I was in trouble. I perked up seeing the Puerto Rican flag on her desk, guessing she was friends with Ms. Rodriguez, and hoped she'd be as nice.

"*Usted habla español?*" I asked her.

"You missed weeks of school. Where were you? You have a tan," she replied in Spanish. She had short hair and looked like she was in her thirties, Mom's age. So she'd noticed my absence too. Had she and Ms. Rodriguez talked about me?

"I had to go see my grandparents in the Dominican Republic," I said, psyched to have two Spanish-speaking teachers, kind of glad they were keeping track of whether I showed up or not.

"You can't miss that many school days," she told me. "I've been calling your home, nobody answers. I even wrote a letter to your folks."

"It's probably in the stack of bills on the table," I told her. "My parents hardly know English. I try to translate, but we've been having a rough time."

"I'm sorry to hear that. Do you want to tell me what's going on?"

"Dad got stabbed twice. The last time he was in a coma and almost died. My parents fight all the time. My brother switched schools and works late so I rarely see him anymore. The other students make fun of my accent. I wanted translations from Ms. Wilson, but she keeps giving me detentions. If I ask her in Spanish to repeat a word, she thinks I'm cursing her." I spilled everything quickly.

"I'll talk to her and your other teachers for you," she offered. "Listen, there are a lot of bilingual students here, like Juana and Junior. You should spend more time with them. They're in my typing class this semester. I'll put you in there too. And register you for the Upward Bound Program that helps first-generation high school students. You should get a dictionary and a thesaurus. We're going to approach learning English differently."

"Get a what?" I asked, thinking the word sounded like a dinosaur.

She wrote it down for me and I checked one out at the school library. I later bought myself one at the 99-cent store.

I felt like Grandpa's Saint Clara card in my wallet had brought Isabel, Ms. Rodriguez, and Ms. Vega to be my guardian angels. They took me away from my problems at home and made me feel protected here. I stopped my truancies and cut back hours at work to improve in school.

"Ms. Beckman is organizing a day trip to Washington, D.C., next Wednesday. Do you want to go?" Ms. Vega asked one afternoon. "Ask your friend Isabel, she knows all the details."

I hadn't taken the U.S. Government course Ms. Beckman taught yet, but if Isabel was going, I was all in. She'd been helping me practice

English at recess and lunch, where we'd make out on the sly. She kept asking me everything about my trip to my homeland.

"I almost didn't come back," I admitted to her.

"You shouldn't stay there, America is much better," Isabel said. "Because I'm here."

5

Premonition

New York, 1996

THE NIGHT BEFORE MY WASHINGTON, D.C., FIELD trip, I told Mom, "I have to get to school early and I'll be home late tomorrow."

"Okay, Quilo," she mumbled, distracted. She probably thought I was studying with Isabel in the library as usual. Mom had a new job at a Long Island factory making scented candles. She left for work at 4:00 a.m. and didn't get home until dinner time. I didn't tell her where I was going; she didn't ask.

The morning bus was unreliable, and I didn't want to risk being late, so I walked the twenty blocks to school, rushing and taking shortcuts. I only stopped once, at a rose bush, to cut off a red flower. I smashed it into the binder where I'd taken to drawing pictures and writing poems for Isabel, in Spanish and English. My latest lines read: "If I could lie to you, I'd say I don't miss you as the night misses the moon and the moon misses the stars." I'd never read poetry before, but I echoed the romantic lyrics of Dominican singers Antony Santos and Juan Luis Guerra. I knew it was a little cheesy, but I pictured her finding the dried, pressed flower and treasuring it as a symbol of my passion.

I boarded the Greyhound with thirty-five other students. Ms. Beckman, a tall white lady with short hair and rectangular glasses, was taking attendance. I was deflated to catch Isabel already sitting next to Junior. "Bro," I whispered to him, "please switch seats with me?" I was happy he answered, "Cool, but you owe me, man." It was a five-hour drive to D.C., and Isabel and I spent it secretly holding hands and talking in both our languages about books, comics, baseball, Jennifer Lopez, and Tupac. When she fell asleep on my shoulder, I sneaked the flower into her notebook, hoping the rose would be dry by the time she discovered it. But she woke up and caught me.

"Nice surprise," she whispered, giving me a quick kiss on the lips.

We were dropped off near the White House. Ms. Beckman led us on a tour of D.C. We took pictures of ourselves in front of the Washington Monument, Lincoln Memorial, and the Reflecting Pool where Martin Luther King Jr. gave his famous "I Have a Dream" speech. It was crowded with many different groups visiting, so Ms. Beckman raised a white umbrella.

"Follow the umbrella," she said. "Don't get lost."

At Garfield Circle, we stood in front of a big statue of the twentieth U.S. president, James A. Garfield. He was assassinated in 1881, after serving only four months of his term, Ms. Beckman explained. I was trying hard to catch up with everything I didn't know about America. In the Dominican Republic, I'd only been taught local history, and I missed a lot of it because Tony and I were often absent from school when we were needed on the farm. My Brooklyn history class was the first time I'd learned that four U.S. presidents were murdered in office—Lincoln, Garfield, McKinley, and JFK—and two—Teddy Roosevelt and Ronald Reagan—were shot but survived. It was scary to think bad guys could shoot you for doing your job well and that even the government couldn't protect you. I admired these leaders who risked their lives to serve their nations and hoped I could be that brave one day. My grandpas told me the Dominican dictator Rafael Trujillo was killed in 1961, but they said he was a brutal, repressive bad guy hurting our country who was better off dead.

The highlight of the trip was visiting the Capitol. As we made our way to the west entrance, I stared up at the gigantic round white dome in amazement. The closer I got, the smaller I felt. It was like stepping into an ancient world I never knew existed.

"What's that statue on top?" I asked Ms. Beckman.

"The Lady of Freedom," she said. "And they say she faces east because the sun never sets on democracy."

That sounded so poetic I wanted to write it down.

Before I could get out my notebook, Isabel said, "Bet I can beat you up the stairs." We raced up all the steps of the main entrance. Ms. Beckman said there were 49, one for each state of the union, with the last step listing both Alaska and Hawaii. When we made it, it seemed like we were on top of the universe.

A long queue of visitors waited in the security screening area. A tall, dark-haired police officer stood in front of an X-ray machine. He didn't look much older than me. He wore a well-pressed uniform, button-down shirt with ribbons, blue pants, and a cool hat, his name displayed on a tag pinned to his shoulder. I was impressed he was so well dressed. How did he keep his white shirt so clean?

"Welcome, ladies and gentlemen," he said in a commanding tone. "Here's the guidelines for what you're allowed to bring inside and how to expedite the security process."

He had a gun, handcuffs, and a baton on his belt; I wondered if he'd ever had to use them. In my neighborhood people were always getting robbed, shot, and stabbed. It must have been a perilous job to work here, protecting the senators and congressmen milling around with everyday visitors. Knowing there was an armed guard here made me feel safer.

"Please take out everything metal for inspection, sir, including your belt, coins, keys, and watches," I heard him say to the leader of another group of students in front of us.

"We should take everything out now," I told Isabel. "So we'll be ready."

When it was our turn, the officer greeted us with a friendly smile. Isabel showed him her lip gloss, keychain, subway tokens, and mints. I held out my train and bus tokens, a few dollars, keys, Skittles, and two Kodak disposable cameras.

"Let me guess where you guys are from," he said.

"I bet you can't tell," I told him.

"New York?" he asked.

"Hey, how did you know?" Isabel was impressed.

"People from New York have lots of things in their pockets," he said. "Welcome to the Capitol of the United States."

Inside, we followed Ms. Beckman, who described, in a loud, regal voice, the Capitol Building's nineteenth-century neoclassical art and architecture, with a floor area that scanned sixteen acres and had 540 rooms divided into five levels seen each year by millions of visitors from every country. It was built by slaves in 1793, she said. "During the Civil War in 1861, eleven Southern states left the union after refusing to abolish slavery."

In Ms. Rodriguez's class, I'd read about slaves in the United States, shocked that it had been legal to mistreat people due to their skin tone and that Black Americans were only considered three-fifths of a person, rather than full citizens. The Dominican Republic also had a history of slavery. Maybe I'd been young and naive, but I never noticed this level of prejudice on the farm. Appalled, I wrote a poem about racial injustice. Ms. Pecou, my Spanish teacher—who was from Panama—called it "soulful and perceptive" and entered it in a poetry contest that I won. If I'd been alive in 1861, I decided, I would have fought for the North.

In my homeland we called ourselves *Morenos*, which translated to "brown" or "dark-hued," though everybody there seemed the same to me. I'd met darker-skinned Dominicans and Haitian workers on my grandpas' farms who we considered Black. In Brooklyn, I identified more as a person of color since I'd been demeaned for being a non-white immigrant using a foreign tongue. Dad's complexion was so light he was seen as white, while Mom was darker skinned, like I was.

Crown Heights offered a crash course on American-style racial tension. I'd witnessed the hatred between the Orthodox Jews and Black residents in the neighborhood, but not knowing English, Hebrew, or Yiddish, or the background, I tried to steer clear of the ongoing feuds that didn't involve me.

Once I heard my mother call out "Hey Moreno," using the nickname of a Dominican customer of ours we liked. An African American woman who heard us seemed aggravated and scolded my mom. "Why are you calling him a Negro? That's offensive." We were taken aback because we didn't mean anything negative at all; for us it was a fond, friendly greeting. But after that, we stopped saying the word *moreno* altogether to avoid any misinterpretations.

"The Rotunda is 218 feet high," Ms. Beckman said as we walked into the huge circular room located below the Capitol dome. "It's the symbolic and physical heart of Washington, D.C., that Thomas Jefferson modeled after the Pantheon in Rome. The Greek artist Constantino Brumidi used dried paint in true fresco style to make the paintings look like sculptures." I stared up at the highest ceilings I'd ever seen. I'd never been inside anything so majestic before. "It could fit the Statue of Liberty without the pedestal," she added.

I'd only glimpsed the Statue of Liberty once, when someone pointed it out as my plane was landing at JFK, but I knew it was really tall. This "grand vestibule" as it was called was home to many famous paintings that lined the ceilings, depicting U.S. historical events.

The Rotunda, Ms. Beckman went on to explain, had been used as a hospital for wounded soldiers during the Civil War. I pictured bleeding cavalry troops on cots and nurses tending to their wounds like in the movie *Gettysburg*. Staring at the picture of Abraham Lincoln's inauguration, I thought, *I am standing at the site where his powerful arguments ended slavery*. I felt emotional seeing this honest hero on the right side of history, insisting on freedom for darker-skinned Americans, who'd lost his life trying to undo the wrongs of racism. It was moving to be in the place where they determined laws, war declarations, and peace treaties. Only a few months earlier, I had been prepared to return to the Dominican Republic, but standing in this special place filled me with patriotism for my new country. I didn't see myself becoming a taxi driver, cook, factory worker, or farmer like my parents and grandpas. I wanted to be something more, to help make a difference.

Next we viewed the Old Supreme Court and Statuary Hall, filled with statues celebrating Americans from all walks of life. In the House Chamber, congressional representatives spoke. Though I knew he worked in the Oval Office two miles away, I still looked around for President Clinton, in case he was giving a speech or signing legislation. I didn't know much about him, but I liked that he played the saxophone and had a nice daughter who was my age. I kept thinking whatever happened here—right where I stood—affected so many people and nations around the world. I was blown away, excited I got to share this whole day with Isabel, as if I'd taken her on the best date ever.

As we walked toward the Lower West Terrace exit, I scanned around for the well-dressed policeman who did the screening when we came in. I found him still on duty in the same spot.

"Thank you for being so nice to us," I said. "*Muchas gracias*."

"*De nada, amigos.*"

"*¿Tú hablas español?*" I asked, not believing this white guy spoke Spanish.

"*Un poquito,*" he said, revealing a gringo accent, then switched back to English to say, "Want to know something cool? This is where presidents come out and take their oath of office during the inauguration." He pointed to an arch entrance with double doors to his left.

"Out of this tunnel?" I asked, and he nodded.

"Maybe you'll be back here one day," he told me.

"Maybe I will. Who knows?" I said, waving.

6

The Wrong Aquilino

Brooklyn, Winter 1997

BARRAGE OF GUNFIRE SOUNDED. THEN AN EMER-
gency siren went off, interrupted by the principal's voice
booming over the intercom that cold January afternoon my
junior year: "Everyone take shelter—there's been a shooting. Get inside
a classroom now and stay there. Do not go outside!"

Two years before Columbine, we didn't have any plan for school
gun violence.

"Let's keep away from the windows," said my math teacher,
Mr. Diaz, rising from the small desk next to mine where he'd been
showing me an algebra equation. He shut the blinds and moved our
chairs toward the door. We were the only two people in there and I
didn't plan to stay.

I jumped up, heart pumping, rushing to leave. "I need to go look
for Isabel."

"No. You cannot go out there now," he said, blocking the only doorway. "We have to let the police and security guards do their job."

The wall clock said 1:30. I tried to recall which class she had before math that day.

Seeing my desperation, he said more firmly, "Please, come back and sit down, Aquilino." I could tell he was trying to stay cool and not panic. "We might as well keep working."

I tried to follow what he was saying, but I was mostly watching the clock hands move in circles, sweating and wondering what was going on. For the next hour, my mind raced. What if Isabel, Martin, and Ivan were killed? Or my classmates Juana and Junior? I desperately wanted to do something to help. Not being able to do anything made my leg fidgety. I couldn't sit still.

Not so Mr. Diaz, the calmest guy I knew. He was from the DR too, but fluent in English. He pronounced every syllable carefully with no accent. He was around five foot seven, my height, and always wore a suit and tie. Like my folks, he was in his thirties. He was firm and strict but treated everyone the same. Two terms earlier, I'd been annoyed when he flunked me. A fellow Dominican should have given me a break. Then I realized I deserved it, since I'd been truant. I promised I'd do better if he let me repeat his course and asked him to tutor me like Ms. Rodriguez. I needed help, not charity or a handout. He agreed if I'd come during recess twice a week. Unlike her, he only used Spanish when I was stuck. As he pushed me to refocus on the problem in my notebook, I couldn't concentrate.

"Why do I have to take math anyway?" I snapped. "It's not a subject I'll ever need."

"Well, what subjects do you like?"

"I like history class," I told him.

"What do you like about it?" I could tell he was trying to distract me so I wouldn't be scared or worry about my friends.

"We're studying the electoral process," I answered. "And how the president and Congress can declare war."

"How could you count votes from elections without mathematics? How would commanders figure out how many soldiers they need for a battle?" he asked. "If you could be anything, what kind of career would you choose when you get older?"

"I'd be a pro ball player," I told him. "I collect baseball and basketball cards."

"You couldn't keep score without math," he said. "You know the numbers on the back of baseball cards? The players' statistics tell you how many games they played, hits and runs they had, their batting average. That determines what they get paid. In some ways, everything in life has math."

"I'm just going to play the lotto and win," I said, knowing I'd never win this argument.

"Your odds are very low, which you would know if you studied more math," he said.

At 2:30, the principal returned to the intercom. The threat had passed and the police had given the all clear. "You can go home," he announced. "We're releasing you early today."

The doors opened and I rushed out.

Isabel stopped me in the hallway. "Hey, where were you?" She was out of breath, like she'd been running. "I was so worried."

"I was being tutored," I told her. "I worried about you too, but Mr. Diaz wouldn't let me leave."

"Everyone was looking for you!" She sounded upset.

"For me? Why?"

"There were gunshots on the basketball court. I heard a bunch of kids got hit."

"Who?"

"I don't know. But the police came searching for who did it. They thought it was you. I was freaking out."

"They thought *I* was the shooter? You thought so too?"

I was gutted. How could she think that of me? After dating for two years, she knew I was a good kid. I didn't smoke, drink, do drugs. I'd even given up the coffee I'd loved when the school nurse said it stained my teeth. I'd heard of immigrants who'd been deported for selling marijuana and cocaine, stealing, and assault. I wasn't about to risk my future.

"They said a boy named Aquilino had a gun," she told me. "I heard you were playing hoops when the shots rang out. I was afraid you got hurt."

My first name was rare in Crown Heights. There were only two of us at Wingate. I'd been on the basketball court with the other Aquilino after lunch, right before leaving to see Mr. Diaz.

"We were playing ball, but then I left. You sure he shot someone?" I asked. We had Spanish class together. "He seemed like a nice kid. His twin brother is too."

"I don't know him," she said, looking placated.

How could anyone confuse me with the other Aquilino? I didn't look anything like him. He was darker skinned, really slim, and tall, like six feet. Even though I was five inches shorter, I weighed more than him. He was older, from Panama, an aspiring rapper who always had a Walkman glued to his ear, listening to El General and Tupac. He had long chains, rings, gold teeth, and cornrows. I never wore cornrows or dreads or put on jewelry, for fear I'd get jumped or ripped off.

"I'd never bring a gun to school or anything like that," I added, flipping out that two bilingual students I'd just played ball with could be involved with gun violence at my school.

"I knew you wouldn't," she said. "But weird the shooter has your name."

I went over and put my arms around her, and she hugged me. "Are you all right?"

"It was really scary," she said.

"Where are your brothers? Are they okay?"

"Yeah, we all wound up waiting in the gym."

As we walked toward the exit, the security guard, Lou—who was speaking into a walkie talkie—stopped me.

"Hey, where were you?" he asked. "They said the shooter was Aquilino."

Lou was a warm Latino guy who knew me and spoke my language, but now I felt nervous, like I was being accused of a crime because of my name.

"I was playing hoops outside but went to see Mr. Diaz at 1:00. I didn't see any fights or weapons or anything," I told him.

"Where's the other guy, your *Tocayo*?" he asked, like I was responsible for my namesake.

"How should I know?" I snapped defensively. "I'm not his keeper."

So they hadn't caught the shooter yet? If the guard who spoke Spanish to me every day was suddenly suspicious of me, what would the cops who didn't know me do? I was petrified.

A few years earlier, my brother Tony had been detained by the police. It was after Bryant, a gang member, warned the Hispanic students to not walk past his homeroom. "Or we'll jump you." I took the threat seriously and went all the way around the building fast, so I wouldn't be late for class. Tony ignored the threat and went straight inside and was attacked. My brother fought them off, punching Bryant, who fell back against the wall and busted his head open, spilling blood on his jacket. Bryant's mother complained to the principal and the police, despite her son being the instigator.

The next morning, cops came to school to take Tony to the precinct. Then he went to court. We couldn't afford a lawyer. One false accusation from a bully who picked a fight could give Tony a criminal record that would lead to jail—or worse, deportation. It was so unfair since he'd only been protecting himself from being beaten up. He had a right to self-defense. Several classmates corroborated Tony's story.

When Bryant was picked up for stealing a car the next day, making him unable to show up to court, the judge dismissed the entire case.

"Were you involved too?" my parents had asked me.

"No, but they're always menacing Latino kids at school."

"Just stay out of trouble," my father said.

"If I saw someone hit Tony, I would jump in to help him in a heartbeat," I admitted.

"You be careful," Dad warned. "This could have had a really bad ending."

After he was released, Bryant told Tony, "I respect you for not backing down, even outnumbered," and they became friendly. I admired Tony for never allowing himself to be bullied by anyone. But since we were kids, his approach was confrontational and reactive. My way was to hang back, avoiding fights. We were surprised the police investigation was honest and we didn't have to bribe anyone to get Tony off, like others did in the DR. The American law enforcement professionals were fair in Tony's case, recognizing the truth.

Now this false accusation based on my name rattled me worse, since I hadn't fought or challenged anyone. I was just putting in an extra hour to raise my grade, but as an immigrant, I was under constant pressure to prove I wasn't a criminal or uneducated foreigner leeching off the system. No matter how hard I tried to be an upstanding citizen, I could be suspect.

Instead of arresting me, though, the security guard updated me on the whole story: Around 1:15, twenty minutes after I left the basketball court in the back of the playground, a brawl broke out. The other Aquilino pulled a gun and started shooting. Three students were hit by bullets and a young man named Dwight Archer was killed. I didn't know Dwight, who was eighteen and went to South Shore High in Canarsie fifteen minutes away, but I guessed he'd been on the opposing team I'd been playing. I'd literally dodged bullets because I was afraid to be late to meet Mr. Diaz. I was grateful another teacher was looking out for me. It seemed like a sign from God or Grandpa Fillo to stay in school, to keep studying and asking for help.

The next day the newspapers announced that three Brooklyn brothers were arrested: twenty-one-year-old Ricardo Lara was charged with attempted murder, along with his eighteen-year-old half brothers Alonzo Soto and Aquilino Soto. *The New York Times* mistakenly called him Ansuilno. For some reason it bugged me that they couldn't even spell our name right. (Ms. Vega later told me that after they served jail time, they wound up back in Panama, where they found success in the music industry.)

After the shooting, the school upped the screening process. Security guards began using X-ray machines, hand wands, and fancier metal detectors, and they patted us down and checked each bag carefully every morning as we walked in. I didn't tell my parents or my brother about the crime and they never mentioned it. They didn't read newspapers or watch American TV news. Mom was so stressed after the van commute to and from her factory job, she'd just take a shower at night, make dinner, then turn on a telenovela to relax before sleep. I sometimes made the mistake of watching the ten o'clock news, where hearing about all the local crime made me reluctant to go out. If my parents knew how dangerous things were getting at Wingate High, they would have made me switch to my brother's school. But there was no way I'd transfer. It was worth the risk to see Isabel every day.

7

American Express

Brooklyn, 1998

To better myself like Grandpa Fillo advised, I tried to erase every trace of the poor uneducated foreign kid who'd landed in Brooklyn six years earlier. I saw Ms. Vega, Ms. Rodriguez, Ms. Pecou, and Mr. Diaz as a supportive team, like a second family, protecting me. With their help, by the time I was a senior, I'd passed all the classes I'd failed the first time around and applied to ten New York city and state colleges. Living at home would make it less expensive. The better my classes went, the more I studied.

Putting in longer hours at the tire shop, I made decent money. After I quit giving any of my salary to Dad, I stopped buying cheap clothes at the Chinese bazaar and could afford to shop at Macy's in Manhattan. Enthralled by American pop culture, I imitated different styles of cool guys like Joey on *Friends*, *Fresh Prince of Bel Air*'s Will

Smith, and Tom Cruise in *Mission: Impossible*. To look sharp and fit in with the popular crowd, I went upscale with Tommy Hilfiger jackets, Guess pants, and Timberland boots.

I admired the stylish skirts, dresses, and spiky sandals worn by Daisy Fuentes and Salma Hayek, but Isabel showed no interest in updating her look. She wore the same raggedy jeans, faded T-shirts, and sneakers, seeming like a tomboy with no makeup, her hair in a ponytail. A girl flirting with me said, "I don't know what you see in Isabel, she's so plain." I felt ashamed to have a plain girlfriend, and then more shame for even thinking that.

"Can't you dress nicer, wear heels or lipstick, like your pretty cousin Elena?" I asked Isabel at lunch one day.

"No," she said, crushed and angry. "If you want to hang out with Elena, I don't need to be with you anymore." She stood up from our table and walked away without looking back.

I should have followed her to explain that I didn't mean it and wasn't into her cousin at all. But I didn't. She ignored me for a week. It seemed clear we were over. I wasn't upset. Honestly, I felt a little excited to be single again, go to parties, and talk to fancier girls. Yet each time I sidled up to someone in a designer outfit and eye shadow, they weren't as funny, kind, or smart as Isabel. Still I didn't reach out to her. I wanted to forget my past and move on with girls who were less old-school and conservative, girls with fewer restrictions imposed by immigrant parents like mine.

After three months apart, I missed Isabel. What I felt for her was much deeper than slick clothes or lipstick. To make matters worse, she was dressing up more, but not for me. I agonized over how mean I was to someone who'd only been sweet to me. I saw how vain and superficial I'd been, trying to run away from who I was and act like someone I wasn't. I'd made a horrible mistake and needed to apologize.

I bought her heart-shaped chocolates and a dozen red roses and wrote a letter, explaining myself. "I'm sorry I was so stupid. I didn't mean it. I was never attracted to your cousin or wanted you to be like her. You're the only one I've ever loved. I hope you can forgive me."

I took the B12 bus to her house with the gifts and apology, imagining she'd give me another chance to rekindle our relationship. Before I got off at her stop, I was stunned to see her kissing another guy down the block. He looked like a dark-skinned Dominican too—taller than me, and more muscular, with a crew cut. I felt inadequate and inferior and couldn't believe how badly I'd blown it.

Knowing she wasn't home, I rang her doorbell anyway. Her mother buzzed me in.

"I brought this for Isabel." Sheepishly, I handed her mom the candy and flowers, assuming she knew why we'd split up.

"Why don't you come in?" she said kindly.

"I can't, I have to go. I forgot my mom needs help with something," I said. If I didn't leave, she'd ask questions, or I'd start crying.

In school, I heard her new guy was five years older than me, training for the armed forces, with his own place and car. How could I compete with that?

My home life was a mess too. Mom and Dad were hardly ever around, and when they were, they fought. I was even lonelier when Tony dropped out of school to work full-time at the tire place and DJ at night. I rarely got to see him. I recommended him for a gig at a birthday celebration thrown by some kids I knew. Our cousin Edgar—who was in the Army Reserve—helped him load up the speakers. At the party, Edgar did the salsa and merengue, and I tried to copy his moves on the dance floor. I introduced Tony to Karina, a cute, skinny girl from my class. Soon after, they fell in love and moved into their own apartment. They even talked about getting married and leaving the city for somewhere cheaper, imagining more grass and trees. With Tony out of the house, I had more space to myself, but I still had to share the pullout with Cousin Agusto. I wished my roommate was my younger, cooler cousin Edgar instead.

Still, I kept studying, overjoyed to be the first high school graduate in our family, albeit a year late at nineteen. My mother came to the graduation. There must have been two hundred people in the audience. I wore a black suit with a bowtie under my black robe because I'd never learned to make a knot in a regular tie. I didn't even have one.

"I'm so proud of you, Quilo," she said.

Most of my classmates' dads were there. I'd invited my father, but nobody filled the empty seat next to my mother, a sad metaphor for my whole childhood. Still, her enthusiasm made up for his absence. During the ceremony when they called my name, I heard a loud *"Gracias a Dios,"* a rare outburst from my usually shy mom, thanking God. She shouted it a second time when my name was repeated as a recipient of a service award for completing the school's Upward Bound Program, something Ms. Vega had recommended that helped marginalized kids like me graduate.

Afterward, I hugged and high-fived my classmates and we wished each other good fortune in the future. Mom played paparazzi, asking me to pose from every angle. I told her to shoot an entire roll for Grandpa Fillo, though it would cost $10 to develop and another $15 to send the photos express, directly to his house through the post office. I felt like I was breaking through academic hurdles for him and all my relatives who were never given the chance.

Isabel's father saw me and came by to shake my hand. "Congratulations. We hope you continue your education." Given how shabbily I'd treated his daughter, it was generous of him to say.

"I plan to, sir," I said. Spotting Isabel, I excused myself and walked over to her.

"Can we talk?" I asked.

She nodded and we walked outside.

"I really want to apologize for my behavior," I told her. "It had never been my intention to hurt your feelings or end the way we did." I was still pathetically trying to fix what my vanity had broken.

"Don't worry about it." She acted like it was no big deal. "Things happen for a reason."

"I really wish you all the best," I told her, taking her hand.

"You, too." She let it go, clearly over me.

Who could blame her when I was such a jerk? This was the price I paid for being so shallow and insensitive. I'd lost a great girl I wished I was still seeing. At least her older boyfriend wasn't here. I secretly hoped they'd split up and she'd give me a second chance. Instead of treating my girlfriend to a romantic dinner to celebrate the biggest milestone of my life, Mom took me for a strawberry ice cream sundae at Baskin-Robbins.

In July, I heard on the TV news that a man named Russell Eugene Weston had gone to the U.S. Capitol Building in D.C., right where I'd been on my school trip, carrying a revolver. He opened fire, killing two policemen there, before being shot himself. I immediately worried about the nice officer who I'd befriended that day. Later in the week, I saw the victims' pictures in the newspaper: fifty-eight-year-old Jacob Chestnut, who was Black, and forty-two-year-old John Gibson, who was white but older than the guard I met, with shorter hair. The criminal who came to do harm survived, but not the officers who courageously did their job to protect people. Chestnut and Gibson were the first American police officers to lie in state in the Rotunda, and then they were buried in Arlington National Cemetery. I hoped someday I could be as fearless as they were.

Not yet knowing which career to pursue, I focused on my education. I took the SATs twice. To improve my results, I signed up to take the exam a third time. The day before, playing basketball, I smashed my right pinkie and needed stiches and a splint wrapped around three fingers from the emergency room. I didn't want to screw up the test, so that morning I swallowed ibuprofen tablets and removed the splint for good. I wound up with a crooked finger. But at least I'd raised my score and received three college acceptances.

The only school I could afford was Long Island University. Their Brooklyn campus was nearby, at the corner of Flatbush and DeKalb Avenues in front of Junior's Cheesecake where I'd get a burger, fries, and strawberry cheesecake for the same amount as lunch in the high-priced cafeteria. I enjoyed my two-week summer LIU program and orientation. Pumped for the fall, I registered full-time, taking the English and communications requirements as well as drawing, an elective, for a total of twelve credits. Now that my language skills had improved and I knew how to study, I earned higher grades than I did at Wingate, making the dean's list and honors program. I pictured being a photographer, writer, or painter and was flattered when my art teacher even suggested I try modeling. I could do anything!

Or so I thought. Unfortunately, doing most things required cash I didn't have. Working thirty-five hours a week at the tire store wasn't close to enough. Spending all $4,000 of my savings and taking out student loans got me through my first term, but I couldn't afford a four-year degree. I could barely afford my MetroCard and fried chicken wings. I applied for scholarships and grants to pay for the next semester. The few that came didn't cover books or meals.

That spring, on my way home from Intro to Photography, I froze when I saw Isabel coming out of the registration office, carrying a tiny little girl in a pink onesie. I stood there, staring at her.

"Hey! What'ya doing here?" I finally asked. "What a coincidence. Are you in school here too?

"Not anymore. I had to withdraw because I just had a baby," she explained, preoccupied with getting her daughter to take the pacifier.

"Wow, I can't believe it. She's so cute," I said, feeling a pang in my heart. The last time I'd seen her was at our graduation that past June.

Had she been pregnant then? I assumed she'd married the tall muscular crew cut I'd seen her with, but couldn't figure out a way to ask about him. "What's her name?"

"Valentina," she answered proudly, bouncing the baby to keep her happy.

I held the infant as we walked to the subway, thinking I could have been her father if I hadn't been so brainless. It felt sad and surreal handing Valentina back to her mother before I went inside the station, and she went toward the bus stop. We were heading in different directions.

"Good to see you. Take care. Don't be a stranger," I said. "I still have the same phone number."

I never heard from her again.

Years later, on her brother's Facebook page, I saw a picture of Isabel in a police uniform and did a double take. I hoped we might bump into each other somewhere, but we never did.

8

Getting an Education

Brooklyn, 1999

BEING BROKE WAS DEMORALIZING. BURNING TO FINISH a bachelor's degree, I thought I could put some of the tuition on a credit card, yet I was approved for only $500. To secure other loans I needed my parents' help. I asked Dad for his social security number, what his income was, and if he'd consider cosigning for me.

"They won't give me a loan either," he snapped. "Why are you spending all that money?"

"Can you at least help cover the fees for next term?" I begged.

"This is all I have," he said, pulling out his wallet and handing me a hundred dollars.

"Thanks, but that's not enough," I told him, not taking it. "It's a lot more than that."

I told myself he wasn't being stingy: he had no idea how much universities cost or that I'd need thousands more dollars to complete my diploma. He'd only been through eighth grade, dropping out when

Grandpa Fillo needed him on the farm. Offering a Benjamin was big bucks for Dad.

I knew my timing sucked. With Cousin Agusto living with us, our one-bedroom was too cramped, so Mom and Dad spent their extra income to move to a bigger Brooklyn three-bedroom apartment on Pitkin Avenue, twenty minutes away. Since he could contribute $200 a month for rent, Agusto took the bigger bedroom with an AC unit. I had to settle for the middle windowless room without air conditioning. The guy who ran Dad's taxi company owned a nearby building on Van Siclen Avenue with a pizzeria downstairs. When the couple running it left, Dad decided to give up his cab to take over the lease. Mom borrowed cash from a man who called himself an investor. He loaned her enough at a high interest rate to rent the pizzeria. I hoped launching a business together would bring Mom and Dad closer, but as finances became tighter, Dad's verbal abuse worsened.

One morning as I dressed for school, I was surprised to hear my mother at home. I noticed she was crying. She wouldn't look at me.

"Did he hit you? What happened? Did he talk bad to you again?" I asked her.

"It's nothing. I'll be okay." She tried to hide her face. "Don't say anything to him."

"Stop protecting him!" I was losing patience. "It's not even 8:00 a.m. and look what he's doing."

She finally revealed that a customer complained after she'd accidentally served him coffee instead of tea for breakfast and my father went off, berating her, shrieking, "What the fuck's wrong with you? You're so dumb! Why can't you ever get anything right?" in front of their customers. She ran home, humiliated.

I rushed to the pizza place, barged in, and confronted my father in front of a full restaurant. "How could you talk down to Mom like that?" I yelled. "What kind of man are you, to disrespect your wife at work in front of everybody? You should be ashamed of yourself!"

He was shocked by my outburst. "Who the hell do you think you are?" he yelled back from behind the food counter.

"I'm the son that you're losing because of the horrible way you're treating her," I told him. "You keep it up, you'll be sorry!"

If I didn't leave right then, I would have jumped over the counter to punch him in the face. Fuming, I boarded the first bus that drove by and considered visiting my old buddies and encouraging teachers at Wingate. But that might seem pathetic, returning to my old high school so soon after graduating. What I really wanted was to ask Isabel—or her parents—for advice. Yet I immediately knew it was a bad idea to go backward. College was the way forward, if only I could puzzle out a way to afford it. The number of hours I'd have to work to pay for the credits wouldn't leave me enough time for classes. Ambition was supposed to be a good thing, so why was it jamming me up?

The bus passed a brick building with glass windows. On the awning was a sign that read U.S. MILITARY—JOIN TODAY. The Marines, Air Force, and Army each had a section. I'd noticed the Church Avenue recruiting station before, but never thought to stop in. I flashed to the day in 1991 in Los Limones when a bunch of pals and I watched through a well-off neighbor's open windows as the U.S. defended Kuwait from Saddam Hussein's invasion on a TV powered by an electric generator. I'd grabbed a stick and pretended to be a brave U.S. military man holding a gun to stop the dangerous dictator from hurting innocent people.

I pulled the cable to make the bus stop, got off, and walked into the recruiting office.

A tall, bald, muscular Black soldier in uniform put down the folder he was holding and approached. He looked me right in the eye and put his hand out. "I'm Sergeant Miller," he said.

"I'm Aquilino Gonell, sir," I said, giving him my strongest handshake.

"Aqua . . . who?" He stumbled on the four syllables.

Since my middle name was Antonio, I said, "Just call me Anthony. It's easier." My brother's full name was Jose Luis, but he was nick-named Tony. Maybe I'd wanted to take on his name along with his bolder, tougher identity.

"You got it. Now how can we help you today, Anthony?"

"Would I be able to enroll in the military now and still go to college?" I asked.

"Yes. You can either go into Army Reserves or active duty." He handed me a pamphlet. "Active duty means you'd draw a starting salary of $21,000 to be in the military full-time once you complete training. After thirty-six months, your tuition would be fully paid by the GI Bill."

But I couldn't wait three years to go to college. I wanted to finish my summer term and keep going in the fall. "What does it mean to be reserved?"

"It means you'd be paid for eighteen weeks of basic training over the summer, fourteen days' annual training, with one weekend a month on base. Otherwise, you're free to go to college."

"And the army could help cover my tuition fees this year?"

"Yes." He pointed to a chart that showed I'd be paid $251 a month for being in the reserves while enrolled as a full-time student. "You can also apply for tuition assistance after you return to your home station at a Public Affairs Unit in Fort Totten in Queens, New York."

"What if there's a war? Wouldn't the reserves be the last to go?" I asked, thinking the word reserved meant "set aside for later." I hoped there wouldn't be a war—at least until I had my diploma.

He laughed. "The reserves are sometimes the first called up." He added, "There's also a signing bonus."

"Really? How much."

"Ten thousand dollars," he said.

That was a lot of money for me. It would definitely help me get my degree. "Then I want to enlist in the Army Reserve, sir. As soon as possible."

"What's going on?" he asked. "What's your rush? Are you in trouble?"

"No. I just finished Wingate High School and started Long Island University. My record is clean. You can check it. I just need to leave."

After I filled out forms, his supervisor scanned my papers, saw that I was born in the Dominican Republic, and asked, "Are you a U.S. citizen?"

"No sir. Just a green card." I shook my head, worried that it would hurt my chances.

"In that case, you can only be in the military for eight years. Then, if you want to continue your service, you'd have to become naturalized," he explained.

"What's that?"

"It's the process of becoming an American citizen."

"Naturalized" seemed like an odd word for it, as if it were unnatural to be born elsewhere.

"Do you have identification with you?" the supervisor wanted to know.

I returned the next day with my passport, birth certificate, proof of address, high school transcripts, and a printout of my college schedule. I wasn't leaving anything to chance. I'd never been more sure of anything.

"Okay. Sign here, and here," Sergeant Miller told me, and I did.

"Next Tuesday I'll pick you up at 0800 hours and take you to Fort Hamilton by the Verrazano Bridge, where you can take the ASVAB test at the MEPS so we can assign you an MOS," he instructed.

"What's all that?" I wasn't following any of his acronyms.

"Military Entrance Processing Station and Military Occupation Skills."

"Dude, with my accent any job will do," I told him.

"I'm joining the army," I informed Mom that night. "If I do eighteen weeks of training, they'll help pay for college."

I felt nervous and guilty leaving her since I was her closest confidant; she barely spoke English. I was her translator at doctor's appointments. I helped her fill out her citizenship papers and file petitions to bring Giovanny and Liliana over. I was glad she wanted to become an official American. But between losing Isabel to her husband and Tony to his girlfriend, and the tension at home, I had to get away. I thought of buying a plane ticket to the Dominican Republic, yet I recalled Grandpa Fillo's wise words. I needed to find a way to move forward in this country, and the army was the best plan I could muster.

"You sure, Quilo?" Mom asked.

"First I'll take my finals at LIU to finish the spring term," I explained. "Next I'll go to South Carolina for a few months of training. Then I'll come back to finish college the next semester."

"My little Quilo will be in the army?" she cried, her face a mix of pride and terror.

It cost ten bucks for a long-distance phone card to call Grandpa Fillo to tell him I was enlisting. "It's noble and selfless to serve your country," he said. "But be careful you don't do anything to dishonor or tarnish you."

What would be tarnishing? Drugs? Sex? Not obeying orders? I felt pressured before I started.

That Tuesday, Sergeant Miller picked me up in a Toyota Corolla and drove me to Fort Hamilton to take the exam. I scored a seventy. That only qualified me to work in supplies or be a cook. Whoever heard of a heroic potato peeler?

I was disappointed. Nothing ever came easily to me. Every milestone was delayed because I'd immigrated and didn't have money. I had to continually play catch-up with the rest of the world. My only edge was never giving up and being willing to work harder than everyone else.

"You didn't do well in math," Miller said.

Fuck, Mr. Diaz was right.

"I know I can do better, sir. Can I take it again?" I asked.

"In a week. If you get a higher score, you'll have more choices," he said. "Go buy the Army Services Vocational Aptitude Battery book. It'll help you. It's the same one police officers study for their entrance exam."

I found it at the Manhattan Barnes and Noble next to where I used to buy painting and drawing supplies. Dusting off my old notebooks from tutoring with Mr. Diaz, I studied hard for five days straight. When I took the test again, I earned an eighty-five. That qualified me for Legal, Personnel Administration, Infantry, or Military Police. Since I'd never even held a gun, I picked Personnel Administration. It finally felt like I had real options.

My hours playing basketball and lifting heavy tires at the auto shop paid off when I aced the fitness test. After I was cleared by two doctors for physical and mental strength, I was told I could start training over the summer, following my school term. To prepare, I took to running back and forth to work at the tire shop, seven miles a day, and to save money, I stayed living at home until I finished college, except for the monthly military training.

On June 13, I was in the middle of a test at Long Island University when Sergeant Miller called me on my cell phone. "Why aren't you at Fort Hamilton?" he asked.

"What are you talking about? I'm at LIU."

"The army bus is waiting for you at Fort Hamilton MEPS," he said.

"I told you I needed to take my finals first." I was confused, sure I'd let him know when my school semester ended. "I already paid for a full term and have to finish."

"That's just great." He seemed sarcastic. "Then you start basic training July 23."

"Can't it wait until after my birthday?" I asked. "I'm turning 21."

"Look, that's the only training course left for the summer." He sounded impatient. "You already missed one round. You signed up, so you gotta go or you'll be AWOL."

"What's that?"

"Absent without leave. You signed a contract with the United States government. Breaking it would mess up everything—your credit rating, your future work standing, and the rest of your life. You won't even be able to get a job at McDonald's."

Welcome to the U.S. Army.

9

Soldiering On

South Carolina, 1999

"YOU GOT TEN SECONDS TO GET OFF MY BUS AND LINE up outside the building by the flagpole. Let's go! Let's go! Get the fuck out of there!" the drill sergeants yelled.

It had been a quiet ride to Fort Jackson in Charleston, South Carolina, with sixty other recruits my age, half men, half women. I'd counted five who looked Hispanic, two Asian, twenty Black, the rest white. "I guess we're the Latino squad," I told the cute girls behind me, Christina Lopez and Carmen Rios. They laughed, but the amusement was short-lived.

The minute we reached the base, six sergeants marched onto our bus, shouting in all directions. We were tired and hungry from the long trip. Lisa, the Black female recruit next to me, fumbled with her luggage, overwhelmed by the sudden rush. The sergeants caught her hesitation and screamed at her, "Get the hell off. Hurry up! Your mommy and daddy can't help you now." Running off the bus with just one of her duffel bags, she tripped and fell, crying as some of her clothes scattered on the ground. I felt sorry for her.

"Take all your shit with you!" a bald white sergeant hollered, grabbing her other bag and tossing it out the bus window. "Get your ass up! What the fuck is your problem?" he asked, making her sob harder.

"Come on, I got you," I whispered, picking up Lisa's stuff, carrying my two duffel bags and backpack, along with hers balanced over my shoulder. I dropped everything off at the flagpole, then went back to help her a second time.

"What the hell do you think you're doing?" the bald sergeant berated me.

"Just helping out my comrade, sir," I said, nervous to reveal my accent.

"Are you her daddy or her babysitter?" he shouted. "You need to drop that. You're not back on the block. Speak English and stop stuttering."

Just what I'd dreaded, being chastised for the way I spoke. Four different officers with drill sergeant hats surrounded me, barking contradictory orders.

"Pick up her bag," yelled a white female officer in green fatigues.

"Leave it alone. Don't pick it up," said an Asian male officer.

"Why aren't you following my orders? You are disobeying me!" the first one said.

"You need to help out your team," screamed the third, a big muscular guy who kept his brown hat down so you could barely see his eyes. His nametag read FIGUEROA, which sounded Latino.

"I was trying to, sir," I mumbled, hoping that would make him a bit more lenient toward me.

"Who gave you permission to speak?" he hollered into my face. No such luck.

The hazing scene was cartoon-like, recalling the sadistic brass in *Full Metal Jacket* and *A Few Good Men*. I was addled, like they were trying to trick me, and completely at a loss as to how to respond. Another recruit attempting to comply with all their orders was demeaned even more. So I stood still, staring ahead, silently taking their abuse, already regretting my decision to enlist. What had I gotten myself into? Unfortunately, it was too late to reconsider. Unable to get a reaction out of me, they went on to torment someone else. Everyone was scurrying around to decipher their mandates. Angry that a few recruits were left behind, a different sergeant made us do push-ups, sit-ups, and jumping jacks. The officers went on with their intentional nastiness, trying to scare us and break our will, to see who they could weed out and which ones of us would be strong enough to make good soldiers.

"You're not civilians anymore," one shouted. "Get that through your head. We're going to get rid of all your bad habits."

They ordered us to do ninety more minutes of exercise in the sweltering heat. We crab-walked with ants and mud on the ground, did more jumping jacks, sit-ups, push-ups, and bicycle kicks on our back. Everyone was sweating and panting before they finally let us drink water and go to the bathroom.

"Next time fill up your canteens or you could die of thirst," a sergeant told us, too late.

I was starving enough to eat the terrible veal, rice, and corn chow at the mess hall quickly, making a mental note to carry little packs of salt, pepper, and ketchup with me to spice up the bland food in the future. Then we lined up to have our hair shaved. In seconds my long curls were ruined by a buzz cut. During shakedown for contraband, they went through our belongings, removing cell phones, Walkmans, Game Boys, wallets, and pictures and locked them away in a duffel bag.

"Where in Jesus did you think you were going? Summer vacation?" a sergeant yelled at a recruit. "You won't see this shit again for three months."

Most of the recruits looked mortified. Having grown up without many things—with rocks as my toys—this rule didn't faze me. But the hours did.

"We have to get up at 4:00 a.m.?" I asked.

"You mean 0400 hours, Private Gonell," a sergeant reminded me. It took me a while to get used to military time, counting past twelve on my fingers.

We were supposed to sleep at 2300 hours, but that was impossible with more recruits coming at every hour, opening, closing, and slamming doors, dropping their bags down on the floor with a thud. The next morning, on my twenty-first birthday, I was awakened before dawn to the beat of trash cans thrown on the floor and metal pipes banging against our bed frames.

"Make sure to fill your two canteens," I reminded everyone. Since a few didn't have enough water, we were "smoked," punished to exhaustion by two hours of calisthenics. One recruit puked on herself; another fainted and had to be revived.

Sergeant Willingham, an older Black officer, let me use the pay phone once to call Mom, warning that I wouldn't be afforded the privilege for the next eighteen weeks. "I'm at the base. I'm okay but can't call you until December." I gave her the number of the base but told her to call only in case of emergency. It would be the longest time I'd go without speaking to my mother. I worried she'd be mistreated by my father without me there to protect her.

We were taken to a medical clinic, lined up, and each given shots in both arms—seven in total—to prevent hepatitis, meningococcal disease, measles, mumps, rubella, polio, and the flu. An hour later, when I tried to pee, my penis had shrunk. A fellow soldier shared the same reaction.

"What the fuck did they give us? Forced birth control?" I asked, only half kidding.

"Maybe they don't want to us having sex?" a soldier asked.

"Or knocking anyone up?" added another.

"Might just be swelling or a side effect," said Sergeant Willingham. "The shots will keep you from getting sick. It's for your protection." He sounded sympathetic as he explained the rules, levels of ranks, who to salute, and what the punishments were for breaking the law and going AWOL. If we did, we would be prosecuted under the Uniform Code of Military Justice, he warned, which was often harsher than the civilian system.

The second morning, an ambulance took someone from the next building to the hospital. He had tried to kill himself. I heard rumors of recruits from the past who were homesick, afraid, and died by suicide, hanging themselves with metal hangers or bed linens. Some had parents who forced them to enlist against their will, thinking the military might fix their attitude. Maybe having a difficult, uncommunicative father and two grandfathers who were tough taskmasters on the farm had prepared me for the army. I was used to navigating Dad's and my grandpas' inconsistent moods and being chastised or blamed for other people's fuckups. So I was less intimidated by the callous treatment from the officers.

The one upside to this bizarre authoritarian universe was having so many young female comrades in khaki flirt with me, taking my mind off of Isabel. While the female sleeping areas were in a different building, we were allowed to fraternize in public. Lucy, a tall, brunette Texan, smiled at me. Marching face-to-face, she winked, throwing kisses. Walking by one day, she intentionally caressed my hand. Sneaking a real kiss without getting caught became an exciting game, but we were never alone, and she graduated training before me. We exchanged addresses and wrote letters. I'd spray my Nautica cologne on the paper; her stationery smelled of Victoria's Secret's pear scent.

During a break one afternoon, Sophia, a petite blond Oklahoman, saw me writing poetry and asked to read it. She wrote poems too. We ate meals together. In September, they began to offer us entertainment at night. Sophia and I made out on the sly while bowling, at the movies, and at a concert on base that wasn't canceled despite pouring rain. When it cleared up, there was a romantic rainbow in the sky. Unfortunately, Sophia was still stuck on her boyfriend back home and not ready to be intimate with anyone else.

At Wingate High, the girls I knew were Black, Hispanic, or immigrants like me. Here, I was catching the eye of white U.S.-born women who weren't my type, perhaps because I'd never met any before. Although I didn't find my buzz cut flattering and other soldiers were taller, I noticed my reflection was getting leaner and more muscular. I wondered if that explained the attention. Then I decided they were drawn to me because I was chivalrous. The other guys could be pigs, racist, and sexist. One white recruit overheard me talking in Spanish to Private Lopez and yelled, "Hey Wetback, you're in America now, speak English."

"I hooked up with Diane from Second Squad behind the bushes today," a soldier told the whole barrack one night. "She sucked my dick without even knowing my name. What a slut." Others jumped in to fuck and tell. Another guy caught in bed with two soldiers in the women's quarters claimed he'd been sleepwalking when they'd both raped him. He was thrown out of the army.

At concerts, if these male recruits wanted to dance, they'd sidle up to a female recruit and grind into her back, stealing kisses without permission. I never made the first move. If someone approached me, I'd ask for a dance or a kiss. I opened doors and treated for dates. All I had to do to stand out was act like a gentleman.

In October, we were allowed to go on our first three-day leave outside the base. A bunch of us booked a suite at an inexpensive local hotel chain where I shared a room with two guys. When the others weren't looking, Cara, an adorable twenty-three-year-old with short hair from New Jersey, sidled up to me, licked my ear, and let me know she was up for some action. After everyone else went out to dinner the second night, we stayed behind for privacy. As she turned off the lights and locked the door, I was nervous. My brother and high school buddies had been with multiple women, but I was still a virgin. Growing up with four strict, conservative Catholic grandparents, I got it into my head that if I slept with someone, I'd have to propose and go through with marriage, and that I needed a job and a place to live beforehand. That clearly was not the case with Cara, who was more assertive and experienced than I was. She had my pants off in minutes.

"I've never done this before," I admitted. "I don't really know how."

"I'll teach you," she cooed, pulling out a condom I struggled to put on.

Between the weird sensation of the rubber, fear that my roommates would return to the hotel and barge in on us, and the government vaccinations that I was convinced had ruined my sexual organ, I was on edge. When I heard the door rattle, I came very quickly.

While it felt good, I could tell she wasn't satisfied, and I fretted I hadn't done it right. Before I could offer to please her another way, we heard a key in the door and rushed to dress in the bathroom so we wouldn't be caught naked.

"I'm sorry. I know that wasn't good for you," I told her. "We should try again."

"It was fine," she said.

It wasn't surprising that Cara lost interest. Still, I'd barely thought of Isabel and was thrilled that, at twenty-one, I was no longer innocent. Everything was changing; the future felt promising.

Over eighteen weeks of basic training and two added months when I was trained on an advanced level, I learned to build strength, shoot different weapons, navigate the confidence obstacle course, protect myself from nuclear and biological chemicals, read maps, do bayonet drills, and throw grenades. But there were setbacks. I couldn't understand words like "protocol," "enlistees," "propagating," "deployment," or terms like "rules of engagement." I wrote each one down and asked Private Lopez for help with the pronunciation and definition.

Though I was a top runner, hours in the freezing rain made me wheeze and have chest constrictions, bringing back my childhood asthma. When I allowed myself to fall back and slow down, the drill sergeant who'd stayed behind said, "You can do better. Catch up." I never told him about my asthma, lest I get sent home on medical discharge. Running ten miles a day, my knees became sore. The standard ibuprofen pills I was given didn't help.

Still, I was competitive. "I bet I could do more push-ups than you," I told another private. During kitchen duty, I arm wrestled. I pushed myself in activities that wouldn't further strain my knees. After I earned 287 points out of 300 in the army physical fitness test and had a shooting score of 38 out of 40, a drill sergeant asked to see me.

"Since your test scores are high, we put your name in for the Soldier of the Week competition."

"What do I have to do, Sarge?" I asked, gratified to be considered.

"Practice. You have two weeks to prepare." He explained we'd be graded on appearance, bearing, knowledge of military procedures, drilling, customs, and courtesies.

Ten of us from the battalion competed one at a time that November afternoon in front of the board of five non-commissioned officers. I was the only Latino; eight other contestants were white and one was Black. I addressed each higher-up by name before answering questions for an hour. At the end, I was called back in.

"Private Gonell, you scored the highest of all your peers, making you Soldier of the Week for your battalion," Sergeant Willingham said. Our commander awarded me a certificate and gold coin I still have that showed an American shield engraved with DEFEND AND SERVE: ARMY PRIDE. They gave me two medals, an Army Achievement and an Army Commendation, to put on my lapel.

It was the greatest honor I'd ever received. I'd always seen myself as an outsider, someone people looked down on or pitied. But now, suddenly, I was winning. I was praised for outperforming peers of all backgrounds, classified higher than average. I joined the army to escape and have my education paid for, yet the military was elevating my self-esteem, teaching me I could be as good as—or better than—anyone.

The next morning, Drill Sergeant Figueroa brought me a copy of the *Stars and Stripes* army newspaper. He pointed to a picture of me standing next to four winners from other battalions. I clipped it to save for Mom.

Hearing I loved art, Sergeant McDermott asked me to paint the battalion's insignia on the barrack's floor, along with a picture of Spawn, a superhero based on a popular comic, who protected his city from evil. I finished the night before I left, painting late by flashlight while everyone else slept. He signed my army yearbook, "Good luck. I hope you go far because you're a good leader. Thanks for Spawn. Stay focused, motivated, and painting."

The army was an equalizer—until family day exposed economic disparities. On the afternoon we graduated training, my platoon created an inspirational song we recited for the brass and relatives who came to celebrate. I felt left out watching everyone greet their parents, siblings, and spouses who'd flown in. I hadn't even asked Mom, Dad, or Tony to come, knowing they couldn't afford the airfare to South Carolina or the time off from work. That day, I hung back with Privates Christina Lopez and Carmen Rios, wondering if they were also from immigrant families with no resources to spare.

On December 15, I flew back to New York. I planned to report to my station, then continue at Long Island University in January. Between my army salary and the GI Bill, I had a little money. Carrying my duffel bags over my arms, I startled my mother at her door. We hadn't spoken in eighteen weeks. It felt good to hug her.

"Why didn't you tell me you were coming home? I'm not dressed nice," she said in Spanish. "And I don't have any food ready for you."

"I wanted to surprise you." I put down my luggage.

"You look so good, Quilo, my handsome boy." She held me close.

In a pile of mail on my bed, I spotted a letter on official stationery addressed to my mother. It was from my commander:

> Dear Mrs. Gonell, Your son was asked to compete against several peers in front of the finest senior officers in the U.S. Army. He scored the highest of all the competitors and was deemed the winner. His accomplishments are keeping with the highest level of service possible. I see his victory as the beginning of a successful military career. Congratulations.

I translated for Mom, who teared up. I showed her the certificate, newspaper photo, and coin they gave me. I was standing tall, in the best shape of my life. I'd lost weight and gained muscle, a solid 169 pounds.

"No more curls though," I told her as she ran her fingers over the stubble that replaced my hair.

When my father came home, he shook my hand and asked, "How are you?" in a courteous tone he'd never used with me before, as if everything had changed.

"I'm doing okay," I told him, feeling more restrained and in control. "Good to see you."

Over dinner I noticed he spoke to my mother nicely, while glancing over at me. I wasn't sure if he was showing a newfound respect because I'd become a soldier or if he was now scared I could take him in a fight.

10

New Uniforms

Brooklyn, 2000

MILITARY ACHIEVEMENTS MAY HAVE BLOWN UP MY ego, but money problems chopped me down. My hope of having the army cover college wasn't quite panning out. The $251 monthly tuition check from the GI Bill didn't include books, transportation, or living expenses, and the $10,000 signing bonus Sergeant Miller promised, that I'd been counting on, never came. I was furious. Now what would I do? Returning to the recruiting station, I found he'd already been promoted and transferred to another state. His replacement wouldn't give me his new phone number or address, saying, "We can't do anything. Sergeant Miller was in charge of your contract and the signing bonus isn't in here."

In my rush to get away from my dad, I'd stupidly trusted Miller and signed on the dotted lines without double checking. Still, I asked my unit commander to investigate. He confirmed: only Sergeant Miller could vouch for me. It wasn't like I could do a Google search.

The internet was in its infancy. I'd have to make long-distance calls I couldn't afford if I was going to track him down. I didn't have the time or wherewithal to unravel the red tape. Instead, I scrambled to combine small scholarships with Pell Grant subsidies and student loans, panicked to think my diploma would be delayed, like everything in my life.

Even more challenging at twenty-two was maintaining my job at the tire shop and army status while I worked as a college resident assistant twenty hours a week to qualify for the grant. That meant I answered phones, filed applications, gave campus tours, welcomed students moving in, and checked them out when they left. I'd report problems to the dorm director, host events, and take yearbook pictures. All this was happening while I had to keep a 3.5 GPA to remain in the honors program. Add to that my parents' pleas when they were short-handed at the restaurant and needed my help with deliveries, serving food, and restocking groceries.

I looked into higher-paying sports scholarships, but I wasn't agile enough at basketball, soccer, or baseball. During a pickup game in the LIU gym, the coach threw us out to make room for cheerleading practice. I was surprised to see four male cheerleaders. I watched as the coach taught them how to lift the girls in the air while maintaining balance. When I asked the coach about the team, he said they could use another guy, revealing that it would pay $3,000 a semester toward my schooling. I tried out and was invited to join the four guys and six females on the multicultural Black Birds. I was the only Latino.

I enjoyed being part of the squad and it instantly made me more popular. In the cafeteria, I ate chicken wings and fries for lunch with my team members Mammud, Nick, Victor, Chris, Radina, Lisa, Alexa, Nicole, Candace, and Syaid. Everybody stopped by to say hi. But I didn't tell my family, wary that their reactions would echo others.

"Isn't cheerleading for girls?" asked my buddy Peter.

"You call that sports?" sneered John, who was there on a basketball scholarship.

"Hey, this pays my tuition," I responded. "Besides, I get to hang out with the cutest girls and travel too." It was also physically challenging, which helped me stay in shape for the army.

My LIU locker became a revolving dressing room for my different identities. Going to class I'd put on civilian clothes, a button-down shirt and khaki pants. Rushing to the army base, I'd change into BDU trousers and green camouflage shirts with black boots that had to be spit-shined. For cheerleading, I'd throw on my black-and-white Long Island University shirt, black pants, and black Nikes. At the tire store, I wore raggedy faded jeans, Gap flannel shirts, and old sneakers I didn't mind getting grease and grime on.

I knew I was spread too thin, but I didn't see any alternatives.

In the service I ran longer, saluted better, and lifted heavier weights than my peers, but at college I couldn't match classmates who came from money and family support systems. I was still supporting my relatives. Though I wouldn't pay for Dad's mistress and second family, I felt obligated to slip Mom cash she'd send to my grandparents, even as I racked up thousands of dollars in loan debt and couldn't pay my own bills.

The first year I'd aced classes, but after my advisor pushed math and science requirements, my grades dropped. Every time I'd get a grasp on schoolwork, military tasks interrupted my flow. I was wasting hours commuting everywhere by bus and subway. I'd beg Dad or Uncle Federico to drive me to Queens, but they were often too busy. My supply sergeant, Ann Merryll, a married Black Brooklynite in her thirties with cool dreads, offered me rides to and from the base. "Let me pay for gas," I said, but she refused. To show my appreciation, after I finished my chores, I'd put in extra hours organizing files for her and unloading equipment, food rations, uniforms, and weapons. But that meant I was giving shorter shrift to academics.

"Hey, why do you get a makeup date for missing another test?" Peter complained one Friday as I was on my way to Fort Totten.

"I'm in the Army Reserves," I confided. "I have to train every month, whenever they call me."

"Oh, that's a bitch, man," he said.

By my second year in the Army Reserve's Public Affairs Unit, I had inched up the ranks to private first class. I was excited when my commander pushed for an overseas trip to Seoul for two weeks that October. Visiting the demilitarized zone between North and South Korea, where in 1953 they'd signed the Armistice Agreement that halted the Korean War, was enlightening. Animosity still reigned. Soldiers were half-hidden and heavily fortified. They kept weapons pointed at each other, as if any moment battles might reignite. The North's horizon was a modern city, luring South Koreans to their side. But it was actually fake and empty, which turned out to be a metaphor for many government facades.

On the way back to the States, I had a long layover in a Japanese airport, so I bought souvenirs (a drawing of Mount Fuji for Mom, a wallet for Tony, and a hat for Dad). If you counted Japan, which I did, I'd now been to four countries: Dominican Republic, the United States, Japan, and South Korea. The world was beckoning.

Despite the angst caused by the curriculum and bills, the biggest perk of college was making new friends. I wished I could live with my classmates in the dorm, but seeing fellow students smoke weed, binge drink, snort cocaine, screw around, and fight—everything but study—reminded me of the fraternity in *Animal House*. Maybe they could afford to party nonstop with parents paying their way. If I did any of that, I'd wind up with a scandal or dishonorable discharge, since the army ran random drug tests during my monthly training. I was safer living with Mom and Dad. Unfortunately, just as Cousin Agusto finally found his own place, Dad took in a new roommate, Pablo, a fifty-five-year-old Dominican taxi driver cousin of a cousin, to help with rent.

Still, it was nice coming home every night to Mom's delicious chicken, rice, and beans, and sometimes she still did my laundry.

Keeping with my late-blooming pattern, I decided to learn to drive at twenty-two. Below our apartment was the Villagran Driving School. They gave me lessons and a test for $100 to earn my permit. I thought a license would help with my commute, but I wound up needing it for better reasons.

"My friend wants you to meet her daughter Natalie," Mom said one day. "I showed her your service picture. She thought you were good looking. She's twenty-one and single."

"Where they are from?"

"Very nice family from Puerto Rico," she explained. "They have their own company your father did business with."

What the hell. I was single too, and lonely. I called Natalie, noticing she had no trace of a Spanish accent. When I asked her to dinner, she suggested TGI Fridays in Sheepshead Bay.

"Sure, my treat. But you have to come get me," I warned. "Unless you wouldn't mind taking the subway on our first date."

She drove me in her Honda Accord. "If you want to keep hanging out, you need to be picking me up," she kidded.

"I will soon. I just got back from basic training. I haven't had time to get my license," I apologized.

She was beautiful in a preppy way. She wore pearls and a V-neck sweater and was taller than Isabel, with longer hair. Over a dinner of sizzling hot wings, shrimp, and strawberry daiquiris, I learned she'd already finished a bachelor's degree and worked in her family's firm. She was more intellectual and sophisticated than I was, traveling to South America, Asia, and Europe for business trips. She was into foreign movies and Broadway shows she'd read about in *The New York Times*. I was a *Daily News* kind of guy. I assumed I wasn't refined enough for her.

But I perked up on the drive back from dinner when she said, "You see that exit 10 on the Belt Parkway? That's called Makeout Point."

"So why aren't you exiting there then?" I teased.

"Maybe next time," she said with a smile, then changed her mind and steered us to the Canarsie Pier.

It was peaceful, sitting on a bench overlooking Jamaica Bay, listening to the waves crashing. We walked around holding hands.

"This is where I grew up," she said. "Isn't it lovely here?"

I wondered what she'd make of Grandpa Fillo's farm with its outhouse and lack of electricity.

Being a respectful gentleman, I didn't come on to her, which paid off since she invited me to meet her parents that night, along with their adorable Pekingese, Sparkle, who jumped on my lap.

"He likes you. Do you have a dog?" she asked.

"Growing up on a farm, we had lots of animals."

"But not in Brooklyn?"

I shook my head, not revealing we could barely feed our revolving door of relatives.

Her parents gave me a tour of their impressive dual-level three-bedroom, three-bath house with a patio and antique furniture. Natalie's father had been in the military before starting his own business. His three kids all went to college. Her brother was on the police force. They were the first well-off Spanish-speaking family I'd seen up close here, much more successful than mine. It embarrassed me that my father squandered every opportunity that came his way. The owner of the tire shop where Tony and I worked had recently offered to sell the place for $15,000 upfront and $1,000 a month to retire in the DR. Tony and I begged Dad to invest. He wouldn't consider it. Instead, he wasted money gambling and playing the lottery. The tire shop was already worth a million dollars. I was determined to break the pattern of my father's failure, and I was sure getting my university degree would help.

As Natalie's mom put out flan and *brazo gitano* sponge cake, her father poured us glasses of *coquito*, a Puerto Rican rum cocktail, and asked about my future plans.

"I'm majoring in media arts in college, but now that I'm a soldier, sir, the army is opening more doors for me."

I thought it was a great sign when Natalie's mother said, "You're opening the doors yourself. Not the other way around. Never forget that."

11

Motherlode

Brooklyn, 2000

I RESOLVED TO KEEP OPENING DOORS FOR MYSELF AND for my mother. As the oldest girl of thirteen kids, she'd been forced to drop out of school in fifth grade to care for her younger siblings and work the farm. My father barely paid attention to her. Every extra dollar she made she'd send to her parents. It worried me that she was too self-sacrificing.

"Start thinking about yourself," I told her. "You won't have anything for your retirement."

Dad was uninterested in becoming an official American, but she became obsessed with the idea since it would let her bring over my teenage half siblings Giovanny and Liliana, who as minors would automatically become citizens too. I brought my mother a book of U.S. history questions and quizzed her on the answers in English.

"Popular sovereignty, limited government, separation of powers, checks and balances, and federalism are the five principles of American . . ."

"Dah-muckrissy," she answered but mispronounced it, nervous she'd get it wrong, flunk, and miss her chance.

"Dee-mock-rah-see," I'd enunciate slowly. She'd repeat it, like I did with Ms. Rodriguez. I recorded the answers on a tape she listened to over and over, while doing chores, instead of music.

In the spring of 2000, I gave my mother $500 to cover the fees, showed her how to fill out forms, and took her to the courthouse interview. Six months later, U.S. immigration services instructed her by mail to get her fingerprints taken and her background checked, and to present proof of her residency to fulfill eligibility requirements. She studied hard to memorize the American history, civics, and politics lessons she'd need for the citizenship test. Over the summer, she was overjoyed to receive a letter congratulating her for passing, inviting her to be officially sworn in as an American.

"Quilo, Quilo, translate for me," she asked, smiling, so excited she didn't realize that if she flipped the page over, she'd find it in Spanish. When I showed her, she cracked up.

Early that sunny morning, Mom and I took the A train to Immigration Court at 26 Federal Plaza, a high-rise in downtown Manhattan, for the ceremony. She did up her hair and makeup and wore her best outfit: a white-and-blue flowered dress with heels. Having outgrown the suit I'd bought for my high school graduation, I put on khakis, a white shirt, and a red tie I managed to knot myself. It was her turn to graduate and be celebrated for once.

The event was held outdoors. Hundreds in the audience watched fifty immigrants from twenty nations become U.S. citizens. Everyone had the same color scheme. The Colombian woman next to Mom wore a red dress. A tall African guy had a red, white, and blue striped tie. A Middle Eastern man donned a Marine uniform. Each was given a small American flag they waved as Doris Meissner, Commissioner of Immigration and Naturalization, spoke of the power and gift of

American citizenship. I choked up when she ended her speech by saying, "Our country is a richer place to have you."

"Sabina Gonell, raise your right hand and repeat after me," a court officer instructed Mom.

I watched from the sidelines as my forty-one-year-old mother recited the U.S. Pledge of Allegiance and took pictures when they handed her a certificate. Everybody was elated, applauding as the speaker said, "Congratulations to our newest citizens."

"This is the best day of my life. I didn't believe it would happen until I had proof." Mom beamed, pointing to the document with her name. "Finally, I'm an American, Quilo, and I can bring over Liliana and Giovanny."

It was noon, so I offered to treat her to lunch or to see Times Square or take the ferry to the Statue of Liberty, to make the day memorable.

"No, I have to go back to work," she said.

"But today is your day. Enjoy it. Forget about work for a few hours."

"I can't. I'm sorry you're too old to get citizenship through me."

Seeing her make it official demystified the process and lit a fire under me. After all, I didn't want to put my life on the line for a country where I couldn't vote. Yet after taking her through all the steps, I didn't have the extra $500 fee for my own fingerprint and background check.

"Can the army help?"

I hadn't thought of that. I brought it up with one of my supervisors, Sergeant Ramos-Mandell. She expedited the citizenship forms along with my security clearance and had the army waive the fee. When I received the social security card by mail, I found they'd misspelled my first name on the card. I had to return, present my official documents, and fill out the application again to get it corrected.

Mom had only enjoyed her citizenship for a month before my father threw a human wrench into our home, returning one day with the nine-year-old daughter he'd had with Estela.

"This is your sister, Stephanie. She'll be staying with us for a week," he told me casually, as if introducing the child of his mistress was an everyday occurrence.

We'd been in this country for eight years, yet instead of easing us into the reality of his second family, my father simply showed up with Stephanie. I was pissed. My mother glared at my father. I felt sorry for Mom, but since Dad was paying the rent, we had little choice but to suck up our rage.

"Are you hungry, honey? Need a drink?" Mom asked the little girl, sweet and classy as usual.

"Yes, thank you," Stephanie answered in Spanish.

Mom served her orange juice and chicken soup. I stared at Stephanie, who looked like I did at her age. She was cute with barrettes in her long dark hair. I wasn't going to tell Dad to fuck off in front of a little kid. It wasn't her fault.

"Hi," I told her in Spanish. "I'm Aquilino, but you can call me Quilo."

"Okay, brother, I'll call you Quilo," she answered in English.

Worse, without asking, my father said Stephanie would sleep in my bedroom. I was relegated back to the living room and had to move all my stuff on the spot.

Dad never explained why Stephanie suddenly needed to stay with us, but later Mom confided in me that the girl had asked her, "Why did you take Daddy away from us?" repeating the lies of her mother, Estela, who was now living in the Bronx with Stephanie's brother.

The next morning, as I dressed for school, my father phoned. "Come help us. A waiter didn't show up. We don't have anyone else." Mom and Dad were already at the restaurant. Stephanie was asleep. Though I resented being made responsible for her, I woke her up and we walked the three blocks to the pizzeria. She pointed at the fire trucks, police cars, and ambulance out front with sirens and lights on. I jumped over the police blockade to run inside, fearing a robbery, another stabbing, or worse.

"You can't go in there," a cop told me.

"That's my parents' place! What happened?"

When my mother had turned on the oven to make pizza, a gas leak exploded in a flare, causing third-degree burns on her face, arms, chest, and hair, he said.

They allowed me in, and I saw her on the gurney and rushed over.

"What happened, Quilo?" she asked, fully conscious. "I can't see."

"You're going to be all right," I said, reaching for her hand, but it looked too burned and bloody. I touched her leg instead. My father ran to get wet towels to soothe her.

"I don't know what happened," he told the police and the fireman in broken English.

He shot me a freaked-out expression, asking, "Can you take Stephanie?"

I thought my father would close the restaurant and come with us to the hospital, but he didn't.

I had no choice. I lifted Stephanie into the back of the ambulance as my mother was rushed to New York-Presbyterian's Burn Center. Mom was conscious, yelling, "I can't see anything, Quilo! Will I be blind?" The EMT gave her morphine. I tried not to focus on the skin peeling off her cheeks or the smell of burned clothes and flesh as I comforted both Mom and Stephanie, who was sobbing.

My mother had gone from her proudest moment to worst disaster in mere weeks. Enraged, I blamed my father for the accident. The pizza maker and I had warned him many times to fix the pilot light of the stove because the burner was loose and missing a screw. Cheap to the bone, he ignored us and fixed it himself. We were lucky the entire building didn't blow up, killing everyone inside. I also guessed Mom had been upset and preoccupied that day after his belligerent decision to shove his other child in her face.

At the hospital, they rushed her into a room we weren't allowed in. I worried about who would pay the medical bills. I'd tried enrolling my parents in Medicaid after Mom became a citizen, but her application was denied because she was too young and not under the poverty line.

As we waited for updates, I bought Stephanie cereal and milk. It was the first purchase I made with my college credit card. In the afternoon, they let us see Mom. She was on lots of medication and was in and out of consciousness. The nurses had put a blindfold around her eyes and wrapped her up like a mummy from her waist to her head, changing her dressing twice a day.

"Where am I burned?" she kept asking me. "How bad is it?"

Distraught that I couldn't ease her suffering, I reassured her that she'd be okay, get her eyesight back, and have reconstructive surgery, echoing her doctor, hoping he was right. My father, Aunt Victoria, Uncle Federico, and my cousins took turns stopping by that week. I called Tony but he was on a trip with Karina, now his wife, in Pennsylvania, looking for houses. I was not happy it took them three days to visit. With Dad hardly helping, everything fell on my shoulders.

Two weeks later, the doctor removed her dressing, unwrapping the gauze bandages around her eyes first.

"Everything's blurry," Mom commented.

"You haven't used your eyes in two weeks," the doctor said. "It may take a little while to get your vision back."

A few minutes later she said, "Wait, I can see better."

He unwrapped two layers of bandages around her head. Underneath her bare skin was purple.

"Are you ready to see your face?" the doctor asked.

When she nodded, the nurse put a mirror in front of her.

"Oh, my face and life are ruined!" Mom cried, staring at her red, charred skin.

"It's not ruined," the doctor said. "It will just take longer to heal."

"Mom, you look pretty as always, really," I lied, noticing the front part of her hair was singed off. I wondered if it would grow back.

When she was discharged a month later, the nurse and I helped her dress in the bathroom. It was a miracle she could walk, talk, and see.

"Some of the scars will go away if you use this lotion every day," the nurse said, showing us how to apply it at home, admitting Mom had a long recovery ahead of her.

An orderly steered her wheelchair to the front of the hospital where my father was waiting in his car. I helped her into the back seat. After he dropped us off, Dad returned to work. Of course, he left Mom's care to me. I took her to use the bathroom and shower every day and rubbed lotion on her skin. I made her chicken noodle soup, rice, and beans, and fed her until she could feed herself. I drove her to follow-up doctor's appointments. Being a good son was just as important as being a good student and soldier, I told myself.

Stephanie left shortly afterward. Her mother was so upset that my father had disappeared for months that they'd broken up. She decided to move with her kids to Maine. While I knew certain circumstances were beyond his control, I vowed I'd finish school and never be anything like Dad.

Natalie sent a "Get Well" card and big bouquet of flowers to Mom from her and her parents. It comforted me to know I had a sweet girlfriend with a supportive family who had my back. But over dinner Labor Day weekend, she looked down at the floor and said, "My mother thinks I should be with someone who can provide me with a better future."

12

Degrees of Separation

Brooklyn, September 2001

I WAS DESPERATE TO PROVE NATALIE'S MOTHER WRONG by finishing college and getting a great job. After school on Friday, September 7, I took the subway to the World Trade Center, eager to do the first assignment of my Digital Photography class. Using my new Canon PowerShot 4, I shot the observatory deck overlooking the city. I planned to return to take more pics the following weekend. That Sunday, my commanding officer asked me to train a rookie clerk at the regional support center in Queens. I said yes though I was already juggling school, cheerleading, and my mother's care. We needed the extra cash. Two days later, Tuesday morning, September 11, a colleague rushed in, hyperventilating.

"Come quick," he yelled. "The TV just showed a plane hitting the World Trade Center!"

Everyone was silent, in shock. After the second plane hit the tower, my commander gathered a team of soldiers to rush to Ground Zero.

Already on base, trained, and impatient to rescue the injured, I volunteered, but he insisted I do my office job.

"You're administration, you need to start calling our unit to report to duty."

I followed orders. Grabbing the unit roster, I phoned soldiers from our Public Affairs Unit, which proved somewhat difficult as cell service near the towers was down. I also called Mom and Natalie on a landline to let them know I was fine. The subways were completely shut down, so at 11:00 p.m. that night Sergeant Merryll drove me and a specialist from our Queens office back to Brooklyn in silence. I had never imagined this country being attacked nor seen America as vulnerable before. We were in shock as we heard updates on the radio. So many innocent people killed in cold blood. We guessed this meant war. I'd enlisted to avoid Dad and finish college, not to fight overseas, but now my father and my classes seemed irrelevant. This vicious mass murder changed everything for me.

When I arrived home, Mom was asleep. Dad was glued to the TV set with our new roommate Pablo, sharing theories in Spanish.

"You okay?" my father asked. I nodded. "What's happening? What's this mean for you, Quilo?"

"I'm not sure yet," I admitted.

"America was blindsided," said Pablo. "That's what the U.S. gets for meddling in foreign affairs. It backfired on them."

"Do you even know what you're talking about?" I snapped. "Do you have any idea what this will do to me and my family? I might be going to war tomorrow."

"If I were you, I'd buy a ticket back to the DR," Pablo said. "That's what I'm going to do."

"You can flee because you're not in the military. But I would never do that," I told him, disgusted. "You've benefited from being in this country twenty years. And the day we're attacked you want to run away like a coward instead of fighting? Not me!"

That week I was frustrated when my request to join the recovery mission in Manhattan was denied four times. (I hadn't yet read that only twenty people made it out of the towers alive, so there wasn't anyone left to save from the wreckage.) On the subway to the army base wearing full camouflage, nobody had ever noticed me, but now I was stopped, hugged, blessed, and wished good health. One woman said a prayer and did a sign of the cross on my head.

I didn't feel that I deserved attention for doing clerical chores, so I tried to join the Coast Guard. They had evacuated people to New Jersey and were prepared to spring into action in case of other attacks. But when the recruiter learned that I was already in the army, he turned me away. "You can't do both," he said. "Legally you can't be part of two military entities at the same time."

I reached out to my commanders. "Call me up for anything," I told them. "I'll quit college."

"If we need you, we'll call you" was their response. But they never did.

The annual required training in October was in Egypt, with a coalition from several NATO countries. I was glad to be closer to the action. The two weeks in the Middle East with thousands of soldiers from Italy, France, Kuwait, and Germany on an exercise called Bright Star had been planned long before the World Trade Center tragedy. Now the collective rage and grief of international soldiers gave the fourteen days a poignant pull. In U.S. Army uniforms, my team was a potential target. We were on high alert and told to keep our weapons loaded but to close blinds on buses, just in case. I sneaked peeks, taking photos of the fifth nation I'd visited.

We toured the pyramids in civilian clothes with Egyptian police escorts. I went inside one, awestruck that it had been man-made from limestone 4,500 years before. For three days we were put up at a nice hotel in Cairo. I bought Mom a postcard of King Tut and Natalie a cartouche necklace with her name engraved. The immersion into Arabic culture and VIP treatment felt odd juxtaposed with news reports revealing the identities of the nineteen men who hijacked three U.S. passenger planes: fifteen were Saudi Arabian, two were from the United Arab Emirates, one was Lebanese, and the last was Egyptian. But I wouldn't stigmatize an entire nation, people, or part of the world based on a cadre of terrorists. America had its share of bad guys too.

Toward the end, I exchanged hugs, patches, and uniforms with all the foreign soldiers as they smoked flavored tobacco from a hookah and we sang Bon Jovi songs. Like many of my colleagues in the army and civilians back home, I was caught up in a patriotic fervor, supporting the War on Terror that President George W. Bush announced. The architects of the 9/11 attacks were al-Qaeda terrorists led by Osama bin Laden and Khalid Sheikh Mohammad. I understood our president's clear objective: to dismantle al-Qaeda and ruin its operation in Kabul by dissolving the Taliban government. That made sense since the Taliban was sheltering bin Laden and refusing to give up the al-Qaeda criminals who'd attacked us. I was more than ready to be sent to Afghanistan for Operation Enduring Freedom.

Instead, I was ordered back to the United States.

In New York, everything returned to normal. I watched the Yankees lose the World Series and took Natalie to the French romantic comedy *Amélie* at Lincoln Center. Afterward, with her parents out of town, I stayed over at her place. I pictured marrying her someday. But my crazy schedule kept me preoccupied. Our timetables clashed.

"I hardly ever get to see you," she complained. "You're not really available."

"It's not like I'm a slacker," I defended myself. "I'm in school, the army, working, and taking care of my family."

"I know, but you're not even close to finishing your degree," she said.

That judgment rattled me, though I understood her impatience. In high school, I'd resented how my background was stopping me from achieving the American Dream. It was why I criticized Isabel, something I still regretted. Now I was the one who couldn't keep up.

"My parents couldn't pay my tuition the way yours could," I pointed out. Natalie was earning big bucks in her family's business, a ready-made position she fell into.

I recalled that her brother was an NYPD officer.

"I'm thinking of taking the test for the police academy after I finish school. Down the line, I know I'll be successful. I just need a little more time," I told her, trying to convince both of us.

"But you don't seem anywhere ready to settle down."

"Is this your choice or your mother's?" I asked, feeling inadequate, wishing we hadn't spent so much time with her parents, not realizing they'd had me on a time clock, judging me deficient.

"My mom doesn't understand how I feel," she said. "I'll worry about her. You do your work."

To be more successful and useful, I quit the tire shop and clipped a *Daily News* ad for security guards needed in downtown Manhattan. After a three-day certification course, I landed a gig with Bell Securities, who sent me to the Chase Bank on Liberty Street, near the World Trade Center. For $450 a week, I wore yet another uniform: dark blue with a red, white, and blue striped tie. I patrolled the area, keeping an eye on vehicles. "If you see anything suspicious, use your radio to call the police," my boss instructed. For the first time I wanted to *be* the police.

After my shift, I gravitated four blocks to Ground Zero, a magnet I couldn't resist. I stared at the ruins where the towers were still smoldering weeks later, smoke rising from the wreckage. I felt haunted roaming around, stunned that those massive steel buildings were decimated and that almost three thousand people had been murdered. Just days before the attacks, I had taken those photographs from the Observation Deck. I could have been killed. Seeing the fence filled with pictures and names of everyone who'd perished, with flowers and letters left by strangers, made me feel despondent and helpless. Passing by EMTs, firemen, and police, I knew I should be a rescue worker too.

"Is there anything I can do to help?" I asked, offering a box of eight Starbucks Medium Roasts.

"We already have enough people here. It's a restricted area. Unless you have a permit or badge you can't enter," an officer told me, taking the drinks. "But thanks for the coffee."

It felt like I was being denied entry to my calling, which made me want it more.

IN NOVEMBER, I took the U.S. naturalization test in Queens. The administrator, a white guy in his fifties, welcomed me. He wore an American flag pin on his blazer. Photos of his son with a wreath showed that he'd died in 9/11. I felt like asking more but didn't want to be intrusive or wreck my interview.

"How long have you lived in the U.S.?" he asked.

"I've been in Brooklyn since 1992, sir."

"It's rare for young people to say sir," he commented. "You must be in the military."

"Yes, sir. I'm in the Army Reserves."

"Who is our president now and who was it when you came here?"

"It was President George H. W. Bush when I arrived. Now it's President George W. Bush."

"What type of government do we have?"

"We have a federal democratic republic, sir."

"We're done," he said, surprising me. I'd expected more—and tougher—questions.

"If you're wearing the uniform and willing to die for a strange land, you've earned it." He put stamps of approval on my documents. "Thank you for your service, soldier," he said, giving me a small American flag and the address of the swearing-in ceremony, which was in Brooklyn.

Mom wasn't well enough to travel yet, and Natalie was working, so on Thursday, November 15, 2001, 0900 hours, I wore my army fatigues on the subway to the U.S. District Court for Eastern New York, near the Brooklyn Bridge. Though alone, I felt connected to the seventy-five other immigrants there, many in uniforms like me: policemen, fire fighters, army, marines, and navy. Walking the five blocks to LIU after my swearing-in, I proudly held my small American flag along with the official certificate stating that Aquilino Antonio Gonell was a U.S. citizen. In the locker room, I changed back into my school clothes and went to my photography class. "I'm officially American," I confided to my grant supervisor later, the only person I told.

"Congratulations. Now go file some papers," she joked.

13

Reserved

Iraq, 2004

B Y THANKSGIVING, EVERYTHING WAS ON THE UP-swing. After three skin graft surgeries that each took weeks of recovery, staying out of the sun, and antibiotics, Mom was almost better. Her skin was still red, but cocoa butter creams faded the scars. Thankfully she could walk, dress, bathe, and feed herself. Pooling money with Tony and me, she bought plane tickets to fly over Giovanny, who was twenty-one, and Liliana, nineteen. Liliana moved into her own room, while Giovanny slept in the living room. I kept the third, smaller bedroom. Pablo moved out. Our place was crowded, but Mom was exhilarated to have all her kids together in the States, and Dad was delighted to have more help at the pizzeria.

I relished moving up in the army. I went from private, private two, private first class to specialist, each with a small raise and medals for Army Reserve Achievement and Good Conduct. I hoped my promotion to sergeant would add privileges or flexibility, but it hadn't yet.

Impatient and unfulfilled by the security job, I asked relatives and fellow U.S. immigrants I knew to recommend careers not requiring a college diploma that paid at least $50,000 a year with medical benefits (enough to support a family). I researched other public service positions: sanitation, fire fighter, corrections officer, and the police academy.

Tony put me in touch with our cousin Modesto, who'd recently become a policeman in Baltimore. Modesto invited me to visit and accompany him on his beat. During the ride-along, he spotted a parked car with a stack of tickets on it and did a license plate check.

"Why bother with something so small?" I asked.

"The vehicle is here illegally. Six tickets on the windshield shows something's not right." The police dispatch came back on the radio to say the vehicle was reported stolen a week earlier. Modesto had it towed to a department lot where they'd further investigate if it was used in any crimes. He taught me to pay better attention to my surroundings.

My other cousin Edgar was now on the Miami force. I visited him for a weekend and asked if I could ride along with him too.

"I love this job. I protect my community by getting criminals off the street," Edgar said.

He gave me a bulletproof vest to accompany him on a stakeout for an informant doing a cocaine buy. After the transaction, the buyer took off running. Edgar chased him. With no weapons to defend myself, I inanely jumped over staircases and hallways, also pursuing the suspect. As the guy was caught and processed, Edgar said, "Even though there's a lot of crime here, I feel like I can really make a difference."

I needed to make a difference too. In Brooklyn, I clipped out ads in *The Chief* newspaper for city, federal, and state jobs in law enforcement. I told Modesto when I took the entry exams to get into the police academies in New York, Florida, Maryland, D.C., and Virginia.

"There's two different police departments in D.C.," he filled me in. "The city of Washington, D.C., is the Metropolitan Police. The Capitol Police is federal."

"What's the difference?" I asked.

"Metro guards the city. The Capitol Police protects the buildings on Capitol Hill," he said.

Recalling my illuminating high school trip to D.C., I applied to the Capitol Police as well.

I was soon disappointed to learn that I failed some of the examinations by a few points because the math part was too complicated for me. I hoped they'd let me take the test again, like my old teacher, Mr. Diaz. Before I could follow up to ask, I received a message from Sergeant Ramos-Mandell: "Heads up. You're about to be transferred to a mobilizing unit. They'll be sending you orders today." I was being deployed to the Middle East!

It felt like a sucker punch. I was mired in mixed feelings. Wanting to see the 9/11 terrorists punished and find justice for the families of victims, I'd kept volunteering to go overseas. The idea of courage, sacrifice, and avenging the slaughter of innocent Americans gripped me. Yet by this time in 2003, President Bush's conflicting political theories had put a damper on my enthusiasm and made me skeptical. After targeting the Taliban, al-Qaeda, and Osama bin Laden in Afghanistan, he'd shifted the blame to Iraqi dictator Saddam Hussein. I wasn't as gung-ho to join an operation not connected to bin Laden or the terrorists responsible for killing 2,977 civilians on U.S. soil. Bush's thin claims that an Iraqi intelligence agent met with a September 11 hijacker five months before the attacks and that Iraq had weapons of mass destruction (nuclear, biological, chemical) were debatable, sparking anti-war protests around the globe. If I wasn't a new citizen in the military, I might have also protested this unjustified war. But I didn't have that luxury. I'd made the commitment to do my duty, whatever the orders were.

The contract I'd signed was for six years in the reserves, with two years of inactive duty. Now President Bush, the U.S. Commander in Chief, was calling us up, mobilizing 130,000 American soldiers to fight against what he called "The Axis of Evil." I flashed to George H. W. Bush's Gulf War in 1990 that I'd seen on television from the Dominican Republic when I was ten. Was Bush Jr. just trying to finish what his father started, as left-wing commentators asserted in the papers and TV news? Avenging terrorism seemed clear and empowering; heading into a questionable war zone was terrifying. I went to the Spanish mass at the nearby church. I'd gone a handful of times in the past, looking for a nice Catholic girl. That day I went to pray for guidance, for Mom to heal, and that I'd come back alive and in one piece.

"Bush is sending more troops to the Middle East," I told my mother that night. "I'm being deployed to relieve the soldiers he sent there first."

"I was afraid this would happen. Do you have to go now?" she asked nervously. "Can't you wait until you finish college?"

"No choice. I'm slated to go for a year," I explained. "I'll finish my degree afterward."

I broke the news to Natalie at Makeout Point, the site of our first date. "I'm afraid to waste your time or disappoint you or your parents. I love you, but you should date other guys. I don't want you wait for me. It's not guaranteed I'll come back."

"What can I say to that?" she asked, upset. Like my mom, Natalie wished I wouldn't go, but I had no choice.

"My entire life will be on hold. What if you wait for me another year and I don't return? I could lose my life or a limb or my marbles and come back all messed up. Let's stay in touch and if we're meant to be . . ." I gave her the address where she could write me. I didn't want to hurt her. Yet at twenty-four, overwhelmed and unsure if I even had a future, I couldn't handle more pressure.

Mom made a savory supper of my favorite roast pork, rice, peas, and guava cake, and then Uncle Federico took pictures of me with my folks, Liliana, and Giovanny, just in case. In one shot, the five of us sat close together on the couch. My father, in his nicest navy blue jacket, leaned his head against mine. I looked like his younger twin. If you didn't know the real story, you'd think we were your average happy family. I gave my mother power of attorney, codes to my bank account, and my address, asking everyone to write. Then I called Grandpa Fillo. He said a special prayer for me.

On December 7, 2003, the anniversary of the Pearl Harbor attack that forced the United States into World War II, I was sent to Fort Dix in New Jersey. We were given vaccinations for anthrax, smallpox, and TB that made me sick for forty-eight hours. We learned desert fighting in ten-degree weather, amid freezing rain and snow. Then we were flown to the Middle East. During a three-hour layover in Ireland, we drank sour Irish Guinness beer. Ever the tourist, I bought green, white, and orange Irish flag keychain souvenirs for Mom and Natalie, counting it as my sixth country. Then we all rested on the floor, using our rucksacks as pillows.

Reaching Kuwait, my seventh country, I was briefed on our mission: to relieve the main unit in resupplying equipment. A few soldiers in my unit who were called up didn't show and were marked AWOL, ruining their reputations. A few others found loopholes like claiming they were pregnant or had flat feet. I had flat feet myself but never considered using it as an excuse to worm out of my service (as Donald Trump infamously did to avoid being drafted in 1968).

"I don't want to fight a war. I never signed up for real combat," confessed Specialist Guzmán, a Latino soldier my age, who did show up.

"What the hell. You thought you were the joining the Boy Scouts?" I asked.

"I was just looking for a way to pay for college."

"I can relate." I patted his shoulder.

"I never pictured being sent to fight halfway around the world," he admitted.

In basic training we watched the World War II movie *The Thin Red Line*. I imagined combat was like that, done in the trenches with rifles and grenades. I recalled my drill sergeant telling us, "Train like you fight and fight like you train. If you train half-assed here, you'll do that in a real war." I was sure I was mentally ready.

At the Kuwaiti military base, we lived in long white tents instead of the buildings we'd had in South Carolina or Fort Totten. Two weeks of sweltering heat made me miss Brooklyn snowstorms. It was dull and anticlimactic, until I was taken aback when our captain volunteered us to go to Iraq. After five days waiting out sandstorms, I didn't know what to expect. Commissioned officers like captains, lieutenants, colonels, majors, and generals had more authority and higher pay. As one of many sergeants (a non-commissioned position) in charge of 109 soldiers, I thought I could handle anything. That serenity lasted only minutes into the ninety-minute C-130 plane ride when the pilot announced over the intercom that, to avoid being shot down, he'd do three aggressive maneuvers, dropping from high altitude quickly while shooting flares. My stomach flip-flopped. I grasped the red cargo strap next to me, double-checking my seat belt clip. A few guys prayed. I kept quiet, hiding my trepidation, touching Grandpa Fillo's good luck Saint Clara card in my pocket for luck.

"If you have ear plugs, put them on," the pilot warned.

I didn't. So I switched from using my arms to brace myself from the turbulence to putting my fingers in my ears to stop the discomfort. For two weeks our eardrums vibrated from the pressure.

"Take ibuprofen for the pain," a crew member suggested.

We landed in Balad in February 2004 and were shown our housing in a tent city. Hundreds of green ten-by-twelve-foot cloth and nylon tents stretched a mile across an old Iraqi military base called the LSA Anaconda, some covered with Home Depot blue tape to stem leaks, not a reassuring sign. Inside the tents were dirt, ants, fleas, and camel spiders, who earned their name from eating the bellies of camels. We were the second wave of soldiers to occupy the base, but the army hadn't made many improvements before our arrival. It was a disgusting, primitive mess: no bathrooms, just porta-potties. For sanitary reasons, we had to burn human waste in a steel barrel, stirring it with a rod while mixing it with jet fuel. There were no kitchens or cafeterias, few military buildings, and no protection. It reminded me of miles of empty farmland in the DR, except the signs were in Arabic instead of Spanish. Burn pits incinerated all the refuse, everything from medical waste to tires, body parts, and garbage. Thick black smoke tunneled up, pushed by the wind. The smell was thick and rancid. (I didn't learn the fumes were toxic until I returned home. By then it was too late.)

I'd read that Ralph Waldo Emerson said, "Beware of what you want—for you will get it." After pushing to be a transatlantic avenging hero and landing in the Global War on Terror, I now wished I was a regular college kid back in my windowless Brooklyn bedroom. However, I decided to make the best out of it. Exploring the base, I bumped into one of the first army units there. They were scheduled to leave the following day. They'd installed an old black-and-white TV and satellite antenna to watch during downtime.

"What are you doing with the TV and antenna when you leave?" I asked their sergeant.

"Come back tomorrow. I'll give it to you for $25."

"Okay, I will," I said. I'm glad I did, as our "temporary quarters" lasted for six months. We desperately needed entertainment to make up for the tedium and lack of equipment and planning. One night on the television news, an American reporter mentioned our plans for an upcoming meeting with Iraqi leaders. I immediately notified my battalion commander that our meeting had been compromised. He switched the time. A day later an Iraqi leader on our side told us, "We apprehended insurgents who heard on TV you were coming Tuesday. They had an ambush ready." If not for my quick thinking, we would have lost soldiers. So that old TV was good for something.

The first time I ever exercised my voting rights was from Iraq, using an absentee ballot to vote against President Bush.

14

Everywhere Was Front Lines

Iraq, 2004

I WAS WAITING IN LINE OUTSIDE THE PX STORE—LIKE A makeshift Walmart kiosk—set up in an abandoned building that only allowed five soldiers in at a time. Sergeant Prendergast, an older Panamanian superior I admired, stood next to me, joking around. He was kind and jovial, the type of officer I wanted to be.

"Hey Sarge, can we cut in line? Our unit is flying home in an hour. I just need to grab souvenirs for my wife and kids," said a private standing with two of his colleagues.

"Troops, go ahead. We just arrived yesterday. I'm stuck here a whole year," the sergeant said.

"Thank you." The private hurried inside with his two buddies.

As I went in next to buy M&M's and Skittles, a blast shook me to the ground, rattling everything in the store. Two more booms smashed the windows. Someone shouted that mortar rounds were being fired by Iraqi insurgents. The land siren went off. Petrified, I hid behind concrete at the entrance, yelling "Take cover!" toward Prendergast. I was choking from the smoke that was suddenly everywhere. Stumbling outside, I smelled gunpowder. The three soldiers Prendergast let skip the line were dead. The one he'd spoken to was on the ground, decapitated, his head in different pieces a foot away from his body, blood everywhere. The other two were missing their arms and legs, guts splattered over their bulletproof vests. The sight was stupefying and surreal. Dizzy, I tried not to puke as I counted five other injured soldiers. I'd never witnessed this kind of carnage before. I stood there stunned for a few seconds before I found my voice to yell for help.

"I don't want to die. Why am I here?" asked Specialist Guzmán. He dropped his weapon and helmet and shrieked, "I just wanted to go to school. I can't handle this." He was having a panic attack, thinking he was getting killed. He ran off to the tents screaming. (I later recommended a psychiatric evaluation that sent him home. He clearly wasn't emotionally fit for combat.)

Looking around, I found Sergeant Prendergast, who'd taken cover inside a bunker near the entrance of the PX store. He came out, surveying the scene, dazed and shaken. Seeing the headless soldier and putting together what happened, his eyes teared up. I feared he might feel responsible for the deaths of the soldiers he'd let go in his place. If he hadn't, his own head would have been blown off instead.

I'd been warned about attacks orchestrated by the Iraqi cleric Muqtada al-Sadr, who opposed our presence. I'd heard on the news that the Iraqi army and security forces of 400,000 had been disbanded before our arrival. That gave birth to a group of 20,000-plus military men turned rebels who didn't want us in their country. I knew Iraq was dangerous, but I told myself that we weren't on the front lines and our headquarters would be safe. I learned quickly, however, that everywhere we went in Iraq was the front lines. Two weeks in, we'd already lost men on our own base. I was petrified it would keep happening.

Returning to the tent city, I saw Cindy, a twenty-three-year-old specialist who'd been flirting with me. She was a pretty African American woman from Brooklyn with long dark hair. She was louder, more down to earth, and more athletic than Natalie. Like me, she was an immigrant who hoped the army would pay for her college. She understood the constant strain I was under.

"We just survived an attack. Three U.S. soldiers slated to go home within hours were killed," I told her. "One was decapitated. We could barely find his head. It was in three pieces."

She couldn't believe it either. "I'm so sorry," she said, checking my bloodied uniform for any wounds.

"I'm good," I told her. She held me while I rambled on. "Instead of their families celebrating their return, they'll be receiving their bodies for a closed casket funeral." That was what I'd dreaded could happen to Natalie. How could I keep my 109 soldiers safe? "Boy, I pray we don't go out like that."

We carried gas masks for nuclear, biological, and chemical attacks, but there were no weapons of mass destruction here. Still, the guns, mortars, and bombs aimed at our soldiers were scary enough. Images of those three privates kept invading my brain. I stayed busy, trying to block the memory of that poor headless soldier.

Seeing Cindy every day that spring helped. She lived in a tent with three other women who switched off bringing home male friends. With my digital Canon PowerShot, I'd become the official photographer for our company. I showed her pictures I took, and she posed for me in different hats and outfits. When she saw photographs of me and Natalie on my laptop, I confessed I still had feelings for my ex, though we'd hardly been in touch since I'd left. Cindy just wanted to have fun and wasn't ready to settle down or get serious with anyone anyway, she assured me. We started tent-hopping, having quickies when we could sneak away.

The army built up the base. By May, there were Burger King and Pizza Hut trailers and a movie theater, gym, and swimming pool.

These amenities were constructed by Iraqi and Filipino contractors who were paid five dollars a day. American engineers set up a satellite station so we could make phone calls and send email. I called my mom every few weeks, complaining that nobody in my family was writing to me or sending me packages like the other guys.

I took it as a positive sign when they promoted me to staff sergeant. Then I learned that five different first sergeants had recently quit. One, an early advocate for the Iraqi invasion, dislocated his own shoulder and was evacuated to Germany. Another went to sleep each night at 2100 hours, ignoring everything, no matter what was happening with his unit. Nobody wanted the job; it was too hard to deal with all the deaths and injuries from attacks on base, let alone from an ill-conceived, contentious invasion we couldn't really win.

My troubles and worries were exacerbated in May when I was called into Sergeant Prendergast's tent. "We had a complaint against you," he said. It rattled me to learn in our tête-à-tête that Smith, the current first sergeant, had accused me of having an inappropriate relationship with Cindy. He'd insisted I couldn't fraternize with lower ranks because of the "power imbalance," though the nature of my relationship with Cindy was hardly uncommon on base. It was a mystery why Smith was singling me out.

Sergeant Prendergast stood up for me. "If I had to discipline Sergeant Gonell for this, I'd have to write up everyone here. Even our captain is seeing an E-5," he'd responded to Smith.

It hadn't occurred to me that my connection to Cindy was improper. I was only three years older and two ranks higher than her, in a different platoon. I wasn't her boss, I worked at a different site, I didn't supervise her, and, most importantly, I'd never coerced her into anything. When I asked her if she thought we had an unfair power imbalance, she laughed and said no, insisting she felt no obligation toward me at all.

"Everybody's doing it and I was the one who came on to you, not the other way around," she reminded me. I was pleased to hear it, since I'd come to rely on her as a close comrade I could confide in.

In retaliation for Prendergast's defending me, First Sergeant Smith, a tall, bald Southerner resembling a Teenage Mutant Ninja Turtle, decided to keep me occupied with constant difficult busy work. The next day I had to put in a ten-hour shift guarding the field hospital, filled with Iraqi detainees hurt from attacks. I watched the helicopter land with wounded enemy soldiers and civilians, some missing arms, fingers, legs, others with open stomach wounds who would go to the bathroom on themselves.

My heart went out to Afra, a three-year old Iraqi bombing victim with ponytails who was missing part of her knees, fingers, and cheek on the right side of her face, exposing her teeth. She'd been dropped off, left for the Americans to care for. Nobody came back to claim her. I didn't speak much Arabic aside from basic military commands and *As-Salaam-Alaikum*, a Muslim greeting that meant "Peace be unto you." As a foreign soldier, I felt absurd saying it to Afra as I shared M&M's and Skittles with her and made funny faces so she'd laugh. I taught her to say my name. In training I'd learned how to tie a tourniquet to stop gushing blood and give first aid, but without real medical training, I couldn't do much else to assist. I felt helpless.

First Sergeant Smith then ordered me to do convoy missions interacting with the local Iraqis, sharing supplies and food at schools "to win their hearts and minds." He made me the mail clerk assigned to deliver large packages and letters to our platoon of twenty-five American soldiers working at Abu Ghraib prison (which later became notorious). On the way, I had to field IED explosives hidden inside animal corpses or buried on the roads that threatened travel. I feared Smith wanted me gone.

As I was guarding the base's tower one night with another soldier, we were shot at. Rounds of ammunition struck right below me. We both returned fire toward the direction of the shooting until it stopped.

As far as I knew, the bullets from my weapon never hit anyone. When several soldiers were awarded medals for the confirmed killings of Iraqis who'd ambushed us on the base and in the field, I was secretly thankful not to be on that list.

A week later I drove my captain in a Humvee through a poor rural area in an eight-vehicle convoy escorted by two Black Hawk helicopters to deliver care packages sent to our soldiers. She exchanged my rifle for a handgun in case we were attacked while I was at the wheel. I was uncomfortable since I hadn't been taught to use a pistol, but she said, "Don't worry, you'd just point and shoot with both hands." Luckily, I didn't have to.

As we were leaving, an Iraqi kid asked for a Gatorade. Tim, a white soldier from the Midwest, threw a full bottle at him.

"What did you just toss over?" I asked.

"Just a bottle to the *hajis*," Tim said, using a slur for Arab.

"We don't have Gatorade," I said. "What was in it?"

"Piss, Sergeant." Tim smirked.

In the mirror I saw the kid drinking it and spitting it out. It enraged me. I'd heard that Tim had been mistreating Iraqi prisoners and contractors, keeping them in the sun without giving them food and water. Back on base I disciplined him for the piss bottle, cruelty, and slander.

"Demeaning people in their own country, you're going to inflame the situation, make Iraqis hate us even more than they already do and take revenge. You can get someone killed," I yelled at him. "How would you feel to be called a cracker, redneck, or white trash, you fool? If I hear any slurs or mistreatment again, I'll report your ass and recommend harsh disciplinary action."

Having been the victim of prejudice, it was something I couldn't tolerate from my troops.

Over the summer, we moved from the tent city to rows of white trailers that housed two soldiers each. I befriended my roommate Staff

Sergeant Desir, who was my age, rank, and also from Brooklyn. We had two small beds, a locker, and air conditioning, with separate trailers filled with toilets and showers twenty feet away. No more dust, ants, fleas, or camel spiders. It was a big improvement. We used two bed sheets to make a curtain in the middle for a little privacy.

The highlight of my year was helping immigrant soldiers from Barbados, Africa, and Jamaica and Specialist Ureña—Dominican like me—fill out their U.S. citizenship papers.

"Why fight for your country when you can't vote?" I asked, pushing the army to rush the process so they'd be serving in Iraq as official Americans. They had to travel in a convoy to have a small ceremony at the U.S. Embassy in the Green Zone in Baghdad. It was held at a tent decorated with red, white, and blue streamers. They received their certificates as they recited the Pledge of Allegiance. The experience inspired a few to extend their contracts. I felt like an old hand though I'd only recently become a citizen myself. Halfway through my one-year term, I was considering reenlisting too, since they were offering $10,000 tax-free bonuses. I'd make sure I had it in writing this time, unlike the enrollment bucks I'd never seen.

But Thanksgiving changed my mind and mood when Staff Sergeant Desir and I were assigned Tower Guard duty on a twenty-four-hour rotation.

"There's a white pickup truck that comes, fires mortar rounds from a distance, then takes off. We call him Mortar Mike," a specialist warned. "Be careful."

It wasn't the enemy that got to me that night, it was a fellow U.S. soldier. After picking up meals for the six of us guarding the tower on the holiday, I was ten minutes late.

"Where the fuck were you?" screamed Sergeant Clarke, a Brooklynite my age but one rank below.

"Dude, I was getting you guys dinner," I explained as I got out of the Humvee to hand out each meal. "Burr wanted steak. Jones asked for chicken, and there was a long line for the turkey and potatoes."

"You should have started earlier," Clarke snapped, obviously exhausted from the long shift, irritated that he had to work on Thanksgiving when the privates had the day off. I was just as tense and pissed off, but wouldn't tolerate disrespect.

"You need to watch your tone and don't forget I'm one rank higher than you," I said.

Back in the uncovered Humvee, I told him to hurry up so I could drive him to his trailer. He got on board, sitting in the back. As we drove away, he threw his helmet, hitting me in the back of my head. Luckily I was wearing my helmet. I slammed the brakes hard and he went forward, busting his lip. He jumped out of the vehicle and challenged me to a fight.

"Get back in the vehicle, I don't have time for this shit," I said. "You got ten seconds, Clarke."

When he didn't obey, I drove away. At the Criminal Investigation Division, I reported him and filed a report. He was demoted to specialist and had to do additional duty for fifteen extra days. I could have had him expelled and prosecuted but pressed for him to get less punishment as a warning.

I took my rank seriously and went by the book, aiming to treat everyone the same, ignoring cliques, nepotism, favoritism, or bribery. It enraged me when army men acted condescendingly and treated me unfairly, like my father had. Knowing how much damage that could cause, I aimed to be more judicious than he was. At the end of the tour, I planned to help Clarke regain his rank so he could be fully reinstated. But first I needed to send a clear message: Do Not Fuck with Me.

15

The Army You Have

Iraq, 2004

I T WAS A YEAR OF DISAPPOINTING ROLE MODELS. MY FA-
ther never wrote me or got on the phone when I spoke with my
mother, even when I called them at work. I hardly ever heard
from my grandfathers. President Bush kept claiming we needed military operations to disarm Iraq, free its people, and defend the world
from the grave danger of an outlaw regime that threatened peace
with weapons of mass murder, which was found to be false. During
a press conference, when Secretary of Defense Donald Rumsfeld was
asked why some soldiers had to dig through local landfills for pieces
of scrap metal to supply themselves with vehicle armor, he answered,
"You go to war with the army you have, not the army you might
want or wish you had at a later time," justifying his administration's
flawed military planning of a dubious battle our country was unpre-
pared for.

Sergeant Clarke got the message to quit challenging me, but first

Sergeant Smith stepped up his bullying campaign, sending me to the guard towers again.

"What's the deal with Ninja Turtle?" I asked Sergeant Prendergast.

"He keeps ordering me to do grunt work twenty-four hours a day. I'm exhausted."

"I think he wants you out of his way so he can get with Cindy," Prendergast speculated.

"You're jealous of Cindy?" I confronted Smith. "Like she'd even look at an ancient dog like you."

"If it was the old days, I'd take you behind the tent and beat the shit out of you," he threatened.

"Then one of us wouldn't make it and that's not gonna be me," I told him, clenching my fists.

"Oh yeah?" He inched closer.

"Do whatever you gotta do. You think you can bully reservists because you're on active duty and you're friends with the battalion commander? If you lay one finger on me, I'll walk straight into the Criminal Investigation Division. Just try me, motherfucker," I yelled, which made him back off. Frazzled, I felt like I was going to lose it.

Marching to my captain's quarters, I told her, "I can't keep working like this. Sergeant Smith has me doing all the other sergeants' work. It's not fair. I have to report on every single injury on the base after each attack, deliver mail, and guard the hospital and prison. I can't do it anymore. Demote me. Take my rank. It's stressing me out too much. I'm not getting any sleep. I quit. Make me a private again." That way I could see Cindy and wouldn't have to work with Sergeant Smith.

The captain refused. "I'll talk to First Sergeant Smith when I get a chance," she said. "I hear 50 Cent is coming to the base tomorrow. You should go hear his concert."

"I'd need a whole dollar to stay on," I quipped.

She spoke to Sergeant Smith, but it hardly made a dent. He continued ordering me to work so many twenty-four-hour shifts that I hardly saw

Cindy. One night, staying up until 0100 hours doing paperwork at the battalion headquarters building, I was so tired I wrote "Unite State" instead of "United States." The next day the Battalion Commander caught the misspelling on fifty awards he'd already signed that had to be redone. "I expect a staff sergeant to be able to read and proofread," he admonished in front of his clerks, humiliating me by muttering, "Fucking reservists."

At first Cindy visited me on my assignments, asking, "What do you need? Should I bring you lunch?" Seeing her every day, confiding in her, sneaking away for quickies, and cuddling made the days bearable. When she stopped coming by, I was overcome with sadness.

"There's a rumor she's been seeing another guy," Sergeant Prendergast filled me in.

I heard it was another Latino soldier. Thankfully it wasn't Smith. Still, I felt defeated. Sleep deprived and drained from keeping up with Smith's assignments, I was fuming that his plot to split Cindy and me up was working.

The next day as I went to the cafeteria with Prendergast, an attack blew up two of our Iraqi cooks. The army employed civilian Iraqis on the base to do landscaping, cooking, and translating. Now, fearing these poor Iraqi workers had caused the explosion, several U.S. soldiers locked, loaded, and pointed their rifles toward them. Locals sometimes did pass secrets to our enemy, though most of the Iraqis who worked on the base were just seeking shelter or money. Their lack of involvement became obvious when another round of gunfire hit inside the cafeteria. It was only then that our soldiers shifted their focus to the real threat.

Although my unit mostly didn't engage in direct combat, over the course of the year, ongoing explosions on the base kept me on edge. Each time someone was shot or blown up before my eyes, I had nightmares that turned into panic attacks. Without Cindy's comfort, my stress levels escalated. I hadn't realized she was the glue holding me together. Without her, feeling pent up and alone, I was falling apart. At my lowest point, I called Mom, trying to not let her hear me cry.

"You okay, Quilo?" she asked.

"I'm okay. It's so hot here, a bottle of ice water melts in minutes. How are you?" I was afraid to ask how she and Dad were doing without me there as a buffer.

"Not so good."

She'd never forgiven him for Estela, their kids, or the accident at the pizzeria. It was already hell before I left, and she told me everything had gone downhill. I suggested she let the pizzeria lease expire, offering the use of my credit and the power of attorney I'd granted her before I left to cosign on a new place near Tony in Pennsylvania. That way she'd have somewhere else to stay while she figured it out.

"You're still young. You're an American. You can have a second act," I encouraged her while sinking deeper into depression myself. Why was I always so brilliant with other people's lives?

"When Giovanny took your clothes," she said. "I told him, 'He's coming back. Don't act as if he's not.'"

I blew up.

"Are you kidding me?" I yelled. "Make him leave my shit alone! While I'm out here fighting for my country, he's stealing from me?"

"He's just borrowing it because he doesn't have many nice things and wanted to impress a girl," Mom explained. "I'll tell him to stop. And I'm lighting church candles and I pray for you, my Quilo. You pray too."

After all the energy and money I'd spent taking care of my relatives, you'd think in my loneliest moments, somebody would come through for me and send the letters, pictures, and care packages I longed for. Instead I was delivering boxes and presents for all the other soldiers but not receiving anything myself. It was exhausting that I had to be the understanding caretaker all the time while my needs were once again ignored. Thinking my brother assumed I wasn't coming home made me feel expendable.

In my warped brain, I decided that if I called Mom every day, she'd notice the pattern and freak out when I stopped, knowing something bad happened. So I gave up phoning my family altogether. I tried phoning Natalie but when she didn't answer I pictured her with someone else. Barely sleeping or eating made everything worse. I went from 170 to 150 pounds, my pants so loose they were falling off.

Unable to sleep one dark quiet dawn, I sneaked to the concrete bunker we used to take cover from attacks. Someone had spray-painted the misspelled CELL BLOCK 424: SENTANCE 12 MONTHS on the wall there, a comment on our mandated boots on the ground. I felt imprisoned too, bombarded by ugly thoughts: I hated Sergeant Smith, who'd ruined my relationship with Cindy. The thought of her involved with another soldier made me sick. But who could blame her? My days were long and hectic. I might never finish college. I'd begged Mom to keep in touch, yet my family hardly even wrote. Tony sent one letter with a picture of himself, his wife Katrina, and their baby girl in Pennsylvania, then I never heard from him again. They'd forgotten me. I'd answered a few sweet letters from Natalie but then stopped hearing from her too. Since I'd told her to date others, I assumed she'd met someone else by now. Overwhelmed and isolated, I needed to escape the loud noises in my head.

I loaded my M-16 rifle carefully, putting one magazine full of ammo inside the chamber and pulled the charging handle to the back. I held the rifle underneath my chin and turned the clip from safe to automatic, then to burst. My finger hovered over the trigger. All of a sudden, the ground shook with two booms and alarms blared. For a second, I thought I had pulled the trigger. But then I heard warnings for everyone on the base to take shelter.

Cindy rushed in first. "Why are you already here?" She was confused that I was so frazzled.

"I just needed time away from everyone," I told her, sweating and shaking.

She noticed my rifle was not on safe and was ready to shoot. "Oh my God, Anthony." She picked it up and removed the silver cartridge. "What's up, honey?" She put her arm around my shoulder, pushing my weapon farther away.

"Having a rough time dealing with all of this," I mumbled. "Haven't been able to sleep."

"You have to stop taking care of everyone else and take better care of yourself. Please? For me."

With her there, I felt calmer. I reached in my pocket to get my unit's roster to begin accounting for all my soldiers, but instead I touched Grandpa Fillo's Saint Clara card. Had she been watching over me? I was about to tell Cindy what was really going on, but then other soldiers arrived at the bunker and sat next to us, with no idea what had happened.

"Platoon sergeants, we need a head count. Do we have everybody?" I asked, suddenly able to slip back into the role of leader and caretaker.

After all was clear, I asked Desir to cover all my tasks on his day off. I crashed for ten hours, woke up, took a shower, and went right back to bed. The next day I volunteered for outdoor missions to get away from the base and Sergeant Smith. I made sure to sleep more and spend time exercising, playing basketball on the court, and running six miles a day to relieve my angst until I regained my equilibrium.

In February, to prepare for leaving, we were ordered to disable the firing pins of our rifles and turn in all the ammunition we hadn't used. I called my parents to tell them my redeployment date. I called Natalie too, feeling lucky to be flying home in one piece, with the same 109 soldiers we started with. Because we were continually attacked from all sides on the base, the army considered us combatants on the front lines. On the last leg of my service, I received five more medals for being in overseas combat with my company.

Landing at the New Jersey army base, I was impatient to get home, irked we first had to spend three days in New Jersey for debriefing. I gave back my rifle the first day. Between my jet lag, PTSD, and exhaustion, I completely blocked out that moment in the bunker, but for weeks after I reached for my missing rifle from muscle memory, even without the uniform on.

16

Homecoming

Brooklyn, 2005

BACK IN BROOKLYN ON FEBRUARY 26, 2005, I WAS overjoyed to see Natalie standing next to my mother and father with flowers. She'd driven two hours to Fort Totten to surprise me. I embraced her tightly as we kissed.

"I'm so glad you're here," I whispered in Natalie's ear.

She looked pretty in black jeans and a blazer, her hair long and silky, as if she'd just had it blown out at the beauty shop.

"Where can we take you to dinner?" she asked.

I'd pictured a quiet private meal at home to ease myself back into public life. I was a little on edge, still half in Iraq, suspicious of strangers and unexpected noises.

"How about TGI Fridays?" Natalie suggested. "You used to love it."

"Then let's go there," Mom said.

I took a breath. "Sure. I have a craving for sizzling chicken, shrimp, and strawberry daiquiris."

At the restaurant, when the hostess steered us to a middle table, I instead asked for a booth in the corner, by the door. I sat with my back toward the wall so I had an overview of the scene and would be prepared for sneak attacks, vetting everyone as they walked in, the way I did on my tour. I counted three exits, noting how we could escape quickly, just in case.

When a waiter dropped a tray and a plate crashed, I jumped, vaguely aware how antsy and easily startled I was.

"How was Iraq?" Dad said after we ordered a bunch of drinks, appetizers, and main courses.

"I'd rather talk about you guys. What's new?"

"I'm back to driving a taxi," he told me.

"I'm taking the reins of my family business," Natalie said. She still lived with her parents.

"So, Quilo, what are your plans?" Mom asked.

"I want to get back to college so I can graduate soon," I said. "I only have one semester left."

We made small talk during the big meal that I insisted on treating for. It was better than I expected, a really nice double date. Until after dinner, when I figured out my parents had split.

They didn't tell me directly, but back at our apartment, I noticed that Mom's stuff was gone. Turned out two months earlier she'd left my father and moved to Lehigh Valley with Liliana and Giovanny. They were living near Tony. That night she slept in our extra bedroom. "I have to get back to Pennsylvania early tomorrow," she said. Although I'd encouraged her to go, it was eerie being back in Brooklyn without her.

After dinner the next evening, Natalie took me back to her parents' place. They were already asleep upstairs. She put blankets and pillows on the living room floor.

"What about your folks?" I asked, noting there was no door.

"Dad sleeps like a log."

"And your mom?"

"Don't worry about her," she said, unbuttoning her shirt. "I really missed you."

We woke up to her mother standing above us.

"Do you want some coffee?" she asked, less enthused about my return than her daughter.

ONCE MY ARMY contract was officially up on May 7, I was done with the military. But they weren't done with me. Like the saying from basic training that *U.S. ARMY* stood for Uncle Sam Ain't Releasing Me Yet, a retention officer at Fort Totten attempted to get me to reenlist.

"Only if we're being invaded," I told him.

He had me sign a sheet stating I'd been counseled. I was released from my current assignment and placed in the Ready Reserves (RR), where I could still be called back in an emergency situation for the remaining two years of my eight-year commitment. A recruiter called to tell me my name kept coming up as someone who should do another stint in Iraq or Afghanistan, saying, "There are multiple units that need your skills."

Jumpy and out of sorts, I dreaded being shipped overseas again. Not wanting another lengthy interruption from college and Natalie for a war I didn't believe in, I volunteered for a healthcare unit in New York. They assigned me to the Eighth Medical Brigade stationed near the Verrazano Bridge in Staten Island. Veterans Affairs absurdly denied my claims to treat the battle fatigue I'd sustained in Iraq, as well as the asthma problems heightened by my constant exposure to sandstorms and the toxic fumes of the burn pit.

Reenrolling in school, I noticed that the only Americans who cared about what was going on in Iraq were the relatives of soldiers fighting there and politicians trying to score political points. Everyone else had moved on with their lives, as I wanted to.

I'd stuck to my promise by answering Uncle Sam's call. But I was figuring out the reason most people didn't do the right thing was because it hurt. Everyone strove for the American dream, but nobody warned you about the downside of ambition and valor.

Laser-focused on finishing my degree, I took a full load of summer classes to get my diploma in September 2005. At last, at twenty-six, I was the first of my relatives with a college degree. This time my mother came to my graduation ceremony with my father. He was sweeter since they'd broken up. That little framed sheet of parchment with my name on it cost me eight years, $60,000 in debt, a disintegrated family, post-traumatic stress from Iraq I feared would never go away, and almost my life.

17

Reprocessing

Washington, D.C., Summer 2006

I N THE STACK OF MAIL I'D RECEIVED WHILE I WAS AWAY, there was a letter from the United States Capitol Police saying that they could not process my application. "We were unable to reach you to complete your background check," it read.

With the whirlwind of my military service, I'd forgotten all of the places I'd applied before I went overseas. Pumped to think I still had a chance at landing a job with the D.C. force, my first choice, I called the number on the bottom of the page.

"The reason you couldn't reach me was that I was deployed with the army. I was in the Middle East for a year," I explained quickly, sharing my name, date of birth, Social Security number, and address.

"The recruiter in charge of your application retired," the man on the phone said.

"Sir, can you tell me whether or not I passed your police officer exam?" I asked. Right before my deployment, I'd rushed to take as many tests as possible. Discouraged by a few failures, I hadn't followed up on all the results.

"Let me get your file to check." The recruiter returned a moment later to say I had passed with the test score of eighty-one.

I couldn't believe my luck. For once, I had perfect timing. "And don't you add ten more points if someone is a veteran?" I said, recalling the rule I'd read in the army material.

"Yeah. Those ten added points from being in the military put you on top of the list for the candidates. Can you come to D.C. to update your application next week?" he asked. "You may be eligible for the next class at the Academy. All you need to do is the psychological and lie detector tests."

He sounded much more enthusiastic knowing I was a vet. It gave me a boost, making me feel like I'd followed the right path, after all, albeit a little more slowly than others.

I called to tell Natalie. "Great news. Turns out, I passed the test I took for the U.S. Capitol Police before I left for Iraq."

As a twenty-seven-year-old army sergeant veteran with a four-year college degree and an excellent employment prospect, I finally felt man enough to be Natalie's husband.

"Come with me to D.C. We can live there off my salary and I'm sure you'll find a job in no time."

I imagined small wedding receptions in Pennsylvania and New York, to please all of our parents. Or would she prefer to elope?

Natalie paused—for too long. "But my family and business are in Brooklyn. Why don't you get a job here?" she asked. "My brother's in the NYPD. You should talk to him."

"Well, there's a lot of things in New York I can't be around any-more," I admitted, knowing I needed to get away from certain relatives while she remained melded to hers.

"I can't just pack up and leave everything behind," she said.

I could.

Although I was sad, I wasn't going to beg or force her to choose between me and her folks. She needed to make the decision herself. When she couldn't, I left on my own. It was over. I later heard she was engaged to a guy from Brooklyn.

In late summer 2006, I bought a silver Honda Civic with portable GPS. I packed the trunk with my duffel bags and food from Mom's new restaurant. Then I said my goodbyes. I was sent to Glynco, Georgia, for three months of federal training. Expecting it to mirror the army with group meals and shared bunks and latrine, I was pleasantly surprised to find we were housed in newly built, classy living quarters that looked like a hotel. I had my own room and bathroom. Sweet. I was moving up in the world. We began with twenty-six students— men and women, most in their twenties, like me, a mix of Black, white, Asian, and Latino. I befriended Jose García from Honduras and Vanessa Méndez, who was from the DR and turned out to be the cousin of a high school friend.

Some recruits dropped out the first few days of Hell Week, when they made us exercise three times a day. As others failed or were fired for misbehavior, the class went down to seventeen. Only twelve wound up graduating. I almost didn't.

All the required reading, legalese, and police lingo messed me up. In a session on constitutional law, I was supposed to arrest a suspect for having a bench warrant out against him. Missing part of the lesson and not understanding the procedure, I'd misjudged the made-up scenario and let the suspect go. That apparently was a big mistake. I should have asked the dispatch if the out-of-state warrant was extraditable, a word I couldn't even pronounce. Because of this error, I fell last in seniority in our class ranking. I felt embarrassed, on shaky ground. To remedy that, I lured García and Méndez to form a study group by cooking them beef and chicken *pastelitos*. Instead of partying on weekends with the others, we memorized legal terms and bounced questions off each other. It paid off during finals, which had a written component and tests for shooting, physical endurance, and police policies. I ended up with a score of 80 percent.

The $56,000 annual salary (with full benefits, paid vacation, and sick days) was higher than my military compensation. Feeling secure that I could support myself, I gave my mother $10,000 from what I'd saved during my year in Iraq to lease her new namesake Spanish restaurant, Sabina's, in Allentown. It would give my brothers Tony and Giovanny and sister Liliana—who didn't have college degrees—steady jobs too.

I was proud to wear this sharp yet comfortable new uniform: dark blue pants and shirt, peaked police hat, boots, a belt, handcuffs, a bulletproof vest, and a gun. In the army, I'd had to wear long sleeves to protect myself from the Iraqi sun and carry a heavy M-16 rifle, ammo, bulletproof vest, and gas mask. Here we learned how to use smaller handguns that were lighter and easier to carry in the holster of our utility belts.

"Do you also want to learn to shoot a rifle?" the instructor asked.

"No, I'm good. I did that for a year in Iraq," I told him.

I was the only one in my class coming from the military. Based on the recruiter's enthusiasm, I assumed my service would be viewed as an asset. I never expected it to be a liability. But then, while teaching us when to shoot at criminals and when not to, the instructor—a retired white officer in his forties—said, "Make sure to watch out for veterans who came back messed up, with PTSD."

That stung. I didn't like how he was stereotyping us, like we were all fucked-up criminals, not showing sensitivity for what we went through. By the second time he repeated negative stereotypes about "messed-up vets," I knew I had to shut it down or he'd keep triggering me. I was no longer a timid, broke college kid; I'd been an army sergeant overseas. I raised my hand and told him in front of the class, "I'm a soldier myself who just came back from Iraq and I find that offensive. It's an unfair way to portray everyone who bravely served our country."

"Sorry," he mumbled. He stopped referencing people who'd been in the service altogether, mentioning other kinds of perps to avoid shooting instead.

After finishing three months in Georgia, we moved to Maryland for twelve more weeks of classes, then two months of field training in D.C. There we were taught the layouts of all the Capitol Hill buildings, the standard operating procedures, and where they did roll call every morning. Of the five Latino recruits, only García and I graduated. None of my relatives could come to the D.C. ceremony, but I sent Mom pictures of my gold-plated Capitol Police badge and my certificate.

Once work started, I could well afford to rent a small room from García and his wife on the second floor of their house for $700 a month. I cooked them Dominican food and we went to their Catholic church together on Sundays. But after seven months, he said his father would be visiting soon, hinting it was time for me to leave. I found an $850 one-bedroom apartment in Alexandria, Virginia, twenty minutes from work. I'd never lived alone before. I bought my own bed, feeling very independent—though Mom found me a couch, table, chairs, and nightstand from a Pennsylvania thrift store that Tony and Giovanny delivered to my place in a U-Haul.

Starting work, I was told to report at 2300 hours, 11:00 p.m., fully uniformed, to the Detail Office near the lower West Front entrance of the Capitol Building. I'd be replaced at 0700 hours, 7:00 a.m. I was glad I knew military time since the police used it too. But I'd mistakenly applied for Shift One, not understanding it meant I'd have to guard the Capitol Building from 11:00 p.m. to 7:00 a.m. five days a week (or that it would take me three years of requests to switch my schedule).

In the locker room my first day, I changed into my police gear, a little antsy, not knowing what to expect. During roll call, I stood with my new colleagues as the lieutenant asked the six brand-new recruits to introduce themselves.

"I'm Private Aquilino Gonell, born in the Dominican Republic but raised in New York. I'm a bilingual army vet and college grad who is happy to be here and ready to work," I said.

Everybody applauded, saying "Welcome" and "Let me know if you have any questions."

Another recruit and I were assigned to go on a scavenger hunt to find all the entrances and exits for the twenty buildings of the U.S. Capitol Complex: the House of Representatives and the Senate, the Crypt, the Rotunda, the tunnel entrance, and the Old Supreme Court. I felt a strong sense of purpose knowing we would be the first line of defense protecting members of Congress and their staff, while overseeing millions of annual visitors. Right below the Rotunda, we examined the Crypt, built in 1827 as an entrance. Standing on a dot signifying we were in the center of D.C., I remembered my high school visit and was amazed to be back. I'd come a long way to work in such a majestic place, though I felt at home, more confident and relaxed here than I'd been in Iraq.

One afternoon, a few doors down from the Detail Office at one of our department's snack areas, I saw only Black officers hanging out, checking email on the desktop computers and watching the Redskins football game. In the other break room, everybody was white.

"Is there some kind of segregation going on?" I asked a Latino colleague in my native language.

"The officers divide into cliques of their own choosing. You can use either one," he answered in Spanish. I ended up switching off between the two groups. Equal opportunity, they were soon both making fun of my heavy accent.

For my initial year, I checked bags and identification before visitors were allowed in, doing the same job as the nice policeman I'd met here in high school. Recalling how friendly he was, I made small talk with the maintenance crew and the occasional senators and staffers working late during budget negotiations and debates over controversial bills. Almost every day I volunteered for overtime across the street at the House office buildings, doing doubles over the weekend, increasing my salary to pay off my debts and help Mom more.

One July Fourth I was guarding a music concert near the Botanical Garden, filmed by PBS and hosted by Jimmy Smits, with Huey Lewis and the News, Taylor Hicks, and Jerry Lee Lewis. More interested in Spanish music than American, I spent a few hours talking to my fellow officer Harry Dunn, a six-foot-seven African American from Maryland who used to play college football. He was fun to work with since he busted my balls the whole time, teasing me about my accent, telling me, "Speak English, man, I can't understand a word you're saying."

"Fuck you. You understand that, don't you?" I told him, glad we became friends.

WHILE I WAS guarding the Senate, a few older white politicians regularly complained that their guests had to go through security, or mumbled "okay" when they passed by without looking at me.

Senator Joe Biden wasn't like that. He was always kind, chatty, and genuinely interested in the people he spoke with. The first time we met, he asked me where I was from.

"Dominican Republic. I just got back from the army in Iraq," I told him, recalling that he was one of seventy-seven senators who'd voted for the war.

"Thank you for your service," he said. "It's immigrants who make this country great."

Inviting groups to the Capitol after hours, he acted like a tour guide, telling stories the whole time, talking their ears off—to his guests' delight.

One night, a new junior senator from Illinois named Barack

Obama snuck out of the side entrance of a budget meeting to sneak a cigarette. "How about those Bears?" he asked me after his hometown team won a football game. Another time he asked, "How's your family? How was your weekend?"

"Fine, thanks. Just returned from vacation," I said. "How late are you guys staying?"

"We just need a few more amendments to the bill, then we'll adjourn," Obama clued us in. "We'll probably be done by ten tonight."

Three more smoke breaks later, around one in the morning, he said another senator was filibustering, trying to prevent the bill's passage.

After he became president, reporters took a video of him arguing for the Affordable Care Act where I could be seen guarding him in the background. Grandpa Bienvenido and Grandma Josefita saw me on the TV news in the DR and called to say they were proud. I loved my job, feeling I was doing something important while witnessing history every day.

At different functions over a decade and a half, I provided security for Presidents Clinton, Bush Jr., Obama, Trump, and Biden. Everyone except Trump had shaken my hand, thanking me for offering protection. I didn't agree with all their policies, especially Bush's decision to invade Iraq. Yet I showed respect, appreciating how they each took time to stop and say hello. I worked security for the funerals of Gerald Ford, George H. W. Bush, Senator John McCain, and Justice Ruth Bader Ginsburg. My most starstruck moment was escorting Justice Sotomayor, the first Hispanic judge on the high court, to her confirmation hearings. Knowing she was Puerto Rican, feeling she was one of us, I congratulated her by saying, "*Felicidades*."

"Thank you," she replied in English, so I followed suit.

"It's an honor to meet you and I'm glad you got the job," I told her, and she smiled.

My relatives back home were more impressed when I was asked to take the lead and escort Dominican President Leonel Fernández to a meeting with U.S. Senator Robert Menendez. The next day I had several long-distance calls from family, squealing that they'd seen me on the news.

DURING MY FIRST three years in D.C., every other week I'd drive to Pennsylvania to help my mother with the restaurant. It was an exhausting schedule, and I was looking forward to a two-week vacation in the Dominican Republic in August 2007. Feeling magnanimous, I offered to treat my father to a round-trip plane ticket, hoping it would be a bonding jaunt we'd take together, for once. Yet he claimed he was too busy, driving his taxi sixteen hours a day, with too many responsibilities to take time off. I was angry that he turned me down, though it wasn't just me he was neglecting. He hadn't seen his aging parents in person for eight years. What was wrong with him? It was like he had something essential missing inside.

Flying there by myself, I stayed with Grandpa Fillo and Grandma Andrea for a few nights.

"When I was a rookie cop, I bought myself this suit at Macy's, but I've been working out, getting more muscular, so it's too small on me," I told Grandpa Fillo, handing him the black pants, jacket, and white button-down. Grandma had complained he didn't have a suit and only wore his baggy farm clothes.

"Thank you very much for bringing me a present," he said. "But you shouldn't have bothered. I don't need anything."

"Come on, try it on," I urged.

I was pleased it fit him perfectly.

"Handsome," Grandma told him, kissing his cheek.

I knew he liked it since he wore it to dinner. I drank beer and ate Grandma's tasty *sancocho*, a rustic soup I'd missed, sharing photos of my time in Iraq in my fatigues and then in my police uniform.

"I'm proud of you," he said. "You stuck with it. And now you're seeing the harvest of your labor."

"Had it not been for our conversation, I probably would have dropped out of school altogether and become a cab driver like Dad," I admitted.

"I'm glad that you didn't," Grandpa Fillo said. "Being an American soldier and policeman are very honorable jobs. Help everyone you can. And don't ever deviate from doing the right thing or do anything that will compromise your integrity."

Since the last time I'd visited, they'd moved into a new three-bedroom, two-bath cinder block house with air conditioning in Santiago. My dad, my brother, Uncle Federico, and I put together the money to buy him the modern home. The idea was for him to retire from the farm, but he didn't seem happy with the arrangement. He commuted two hours back and forth several times a week in a rickety bus, carrying plantains, melons, potatoes, and peas in a sack. I saw where my father and I got our work ethic from.

"You should sell the farm so you can retire comfortably in the city," I told him.

"I like the farm better, it's quieter there," he said as loud motorcycles revved up and drove by his house. "Besides I have to look out for my land."

Grandma filled me in on his latest problems: robbers were taking down his fences so they could cut his trees for lumber and steal his crops. He was going back and forth more often to protect his acres. Sometimes, as his own watchman, he'd sleep outside in his hammock with just his machete and dog.

I spent time on the beach in Puerto Plata with Uncle Carlos and his wife, stopped by to see Grandpa Bienvenido and Grandma Josefita, and went to the 27 Charcos de Damajagua waterfall in the mountains that I hadn't seen since I was twelve.

Before I left, I stopped over to say goodbye to Grandpa Fillo. "I love you," I told him, hugging him close. "See you next summer."

Two weeks later, Uncle Carlos called me in D.C. when I was patrolling the Capitol to say there'd been a terrible accident. "The cargo of a Mack truck tractor trailer broke loose. It was carrying concrete pipes that rolled over and smashed the bus Fillo was on." He was seventy-six. I was despondent to lose the only paternal figure I'd ever admired.

I couldn't afford to take more days off work and buy another plane ticket for myself. But I spent $800 for a round trip for my father.

"You should have come with me and spent time with him while you still could," I scolded him.

"You're right. I should have come," Dad said, tearing up.

The first time I went to church in Virginia was to light a candle for Grandpa Fillo and say a prayer, using his real name, Porfirio Gonell. I feared he'd told Saint Clara to watch over me, but not him, as if he'd given away all of his luck and forgot to save any for himself.

18

Dancing in the Dark

Washington, D.C., July 2008

I WAS WIPED OUT AFTER A SIXTEEN-HOUR SHIFT, BUT I didn't want to spend another Saturday night alone. At my place, I changed into an Armani shirt, nice jeans, and black leather dress shoes, then drove to Muse, a local lounge I'd heard about. For their Spanish night, they were having a Colombian Independence Day celebration. I was craving a mojito. The rum punch and smooth Latin drumbeat had my hips swaying.

"Are you up for dancing?" I asked a dark-haired woman at the bar.

"No, sorry. I'm with my friends," she said, turning away.

"How about a little salsa?" I offered a blond lady in a green dress sitting at a table.

"My food just came," she said, pointing to her burger.

"Will you join me on the dance floor?" I asked a third patron near the door.

She shook her head no and left.

After three strikeouts, at 1:30 a.m., I was about to give up when I spotted a beauty with long reddish-brown hair doing a mean salsa by herself in the corner. She was slim, in jeans with a metallic top that glittered, heels, and dangling silver earrings. She had long eyelashes and pink lip gloss.

"I don't know all the salsa steps, but I remember the basics," I said. "Want to give it a whirl?"

I put out my hand. She took it.

She was a graceful dancer, twisting and turning to the sexy beat just like Shakira. It was electrifying but nerve-racking since she danced so much better than me, way out of my league. I could barely keep up, feeling like an awkward gringo. Luckily the next song was a bachata, my favorite Dominican dance. In between the steps, holding hands while moving our feet to the tempo, I managed to introduce myself and learn a bit about her. Monica was a twenty-two-year-old Colombian who'd moved here when she was fifteen. A recent college grad, she was planning to apply to medical school. Beauty, brains, rhythm, and Spanish-speaking! The only problem: her older brother Juan was a strict bodyguard. No wonder he was hovering around us, giving me the eye. At twenty-nine, was I too old for her?

After dancing another half hour, I offered to buy her a drink.

"I don't take drinks from guys I don't know," she said. "Especially when they're drunk," she added, loud enough for her brother to hear.

"I'm not drunk at all. I just worked a sixteen-hour shift, so my eyes look tired. I'm a police officer. I work at the Capitol Police," I replied, hoping he'd overhear that too.

"Really, another one?" Juan commented. "He doesn't look like it. Who the fuck is he?"

I didn't know what that meant. "Can I get you bottled water?" I tried.

She laughed and led me back to the dance floor. By 3:00 a.m. the music stopped and the lights came up, but we were merenguing like crazy.

"Okay, the show is over," the DJ announced, kicking us all out.

"I enjoyed dancing with you. Can I get your number?" I asked, walking her outside to her brother's car, where he was sitting with his girlfriend, glaring at me.

"Well, I have a boyfriend," she said.

It was a stab to my heart.

"He's a police officer too," she added.

So that was what her brother meant. At least I might fit her type?

"Oh, I was just hoping we could dance again," I said, trying to recover.

"I have a cute girlfriend I'll introduce you to," she told me, immediately friend-zoning me.

"Sounds cool, thanks." I lied to get her number, pleased she asked to take a quick selfie with me before leaving. I sure hoped it wasn't our first and last photograph together.

Two days later, I tried calling to see if the number she gave me was fake. It wasn't. After we chatted a bit, I suggested she call me whenever she felt like dancing again, but she never did.

Months later, I was deleting old acquaintances from my cell phone and saw Monica's picture and number. I flashed to her sparkling on the Muse dance floor, felt a pang, and messaged her. "Just want to say hello. I hope all's going well for you."

She texted me back, revealing that she and her boyfriend had recently broken up. I was thrilled, thankful that I had a very persistent personality. A lot of dreams I'd missed on my first go-around came true after I'd asked for a second chance.

"Then can I take you out to dinner Saturday night?" I tried.

She was hesitant.

It turned out that her parents wouldn't let her go to bars without

Juan there to shield her, and Juan didn't have a great opinion of me. He was not so happy that she'd danced with a stranger. Her folks weren't on board either. They'd warned her that police officers and Dominican men were known to be players. So I already had two strikes against me. Strike three was my age; they thought I was too old for her. But I didn't give up. On my way home from visiting Mom in Pennsylvania that Sunday afternoon, I called Monica.

"What are you doing now?"

"I'm with my parents, we just got home from a trip," she told me.

"Can I come over? I'm nearby," I said. "I have a present for you. Text me your address."

Thus I finagled an introduction to meet her mom and dad in the parking lot of her apartment building. After shaking their hands, I opened my car's trunk to show it was overstuffed with my mother's Dominican food from Sabina's: octopus and shrimp salad, rotisserie chicken, roast pork, *pastelitos*, pigeon peas, rice, *sancocho*, and dessert: flan, guava, and tres leches cake. Mom had packed up a little bit of everything for me to freeze, so I had food for several weeks.

"Are you having a party?" Monica asked.

"I just came from my mom's restaurant. Are you guys hungry?"

"We're starving," Juan said, as everyone gathered around the tin containers.

I handed out the *pastelitos* first.

"Wow, this is delicious," her mother said.

Juan grabbed a piece of roast pork from another container. Her father tasted it too.

"Try this," her brother said, grabbing a chicken leg.

Luckily Mom had added napkins. We stood there in the parking lot, eating out of the trunk of my car with our hands, until most of the food was gone. They sure could pack it in. They were just my type: a close-knit, down-to-earth *familia* with big appetites. I won them over during our huge Dominican feast.

"Can I please go inside to use your restroom?" I asked. "I was driving for four hours."

In their kitchen her mother said, "What can I get you to drink?"

"Water would be great," I told her.

"Your mother sure can cook," Monica's father told me.

"If you keep me around, I'll take you all to her restaurant in Pennsylvania one day."

It was a promise I soon kept.

Monica and I married on October 24, 2010, a year and a half after the trunk feast. I was thirty-one and wore a black suit and striped tie. My gorgeous twenty-four-year-old bride wore a short beige dress with matching heels for the civil ceremony in Woodridge, Virginia. Among the third relatives celebrating with us were her parents; Tony, Karina, and their two kids; Giovanny, his wife, and their two kids; Liliana, who'd just had a new baby; and my half sister Stephanie, who was eighteen and wore a lovely silver dress. I was trying to talk her into going to the police academy too.

In 2011, when President Obama announced that United States Navy SEALs had killed Osama bin Laden almost a decade after he'd launched the worst terrorist attack in U.S. history, I felt like justice had finally been served. Yet Iraq remained an unnecessary and tragic distraction.

That same year, Monica and I welcomed our son Emmanuel, giving him a name that meant "God is with us." We chose it because his birth was a *bendición*. Fulfilling the American Dream, I was overcome with joy that after so much sacrifice and hard work, I was able to help my relatives and provide my son all the opportunities my grandfathers, my parents, and I never had.

Acknowledgment of the sixteen years I served

Proud of my badge

Gold Medal signing ceremony at the White House. *Courtesy of the White House*

Meeting General Miley

My mom, Tony, and me in the early '80s

My grandparents Fillo and Andrea in their new home in
Santiago, Dominican Republic

Fillo with his new suit I got him on my trip back
to the Dominican Republic

My grandparents Josefita and Bienvenido. Saying goodbye

Our Wedding Day. Clockwise from top left: my sister Stephanie, my dad, me, Monica, my sister Liliana and her newborn, my mom, my brothers Tony and Giovanny

My first Convoy mission in Iraq, 2004. I took this photo using my new camera

Holding the line against the mob: the moment my shoulder was injured

Still frames from open source videos showing where I was in the tunnel. The arrows pinpoint my location. *Courtesy of the Sedition Hunters Community*

Still on high alert. In my CDU uniform a
few days after January 6

Presiden Biden's inauguration and my last day on full duty

Speaker Emerita Pelosi and me at the American Spirit Awards, where we both received awards for defending our constitutional democracy

Being the role model to my son that I never had

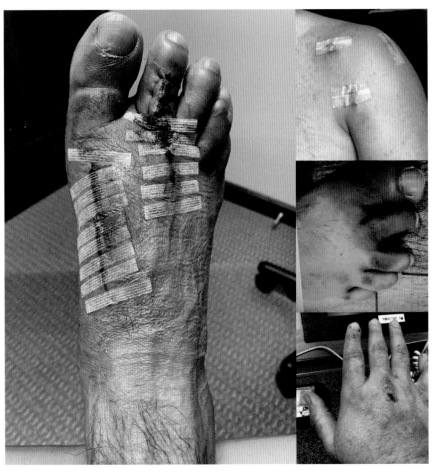

My most severe injuries. Souvenir from the peaceful tourists. AKA the way Trump supporters support the police

Thanking Jon Stewart for advocating for the passage of the PACT ACT and his support for first responders. *Courtesy of Frank Thorp V*

Hopeful for a better future

Proud moment: my son pinning my sergeant badge during my promotion ceremony

PART
TWO

19

Overtime

Washington, D.C., January 6, 2021

THE ALARM BLARED AT 4:00 A.M. THAT WEDNESDAY morning. I turned it off. I was exhausted. For the past six months, I'd been working double duty under pandemic guidelines. I was promoted to sergeant in 2018, which meant I was now in charge of my own squad in the Civil Disturbance Unit. We'd been activated on and off since the summer, due to Black Lives Matter demonstrators clashing with police and Trump followers rallying near the White House. I usually worked the midnight shift, but in case the protests escalated or too many officers called in sick with the coronavirus, my hours were switched. I was ordered to work from 7:00 a.m. to "whenever it was deemed necessary." I was feeling a little disoriented. Today I could be on the job eighteen hours straight, with mandatory overtime, when I'd rather be home with my family.

Knowing I was drained, Monica got up to help me get ready. Milo, our short-haired pointer, woke up and bounded over from his dog bed.

Once I petted the puppy, he went back to sleep. I wished I could too. Instead, I showered and dressed. Despite the darkness and early hour, I loved waking up in our new house in the Virginia suburbs. After a lifetime of small living spaces, this grand three-bedroom, three-bath Colonial was a palace. It had a basketball hoop in the driveway and a ready-made treehouse where my son did his remote fourth grade classes during the COVID crisis, to make learning fun. In the backyard I'd planted corn, beans, eggplants, and other vegetables, in homage to both of my grandfathers. At forty-two, I had a wife and son I adored and a steady job I enjoyed. I made good money working overtime, and I was looking forward to taking the test for lieutenant. I felt like I'd made it.

Only a few days earlier, we'd celebrated New Year's by eating twelve grapes at midnight for good luck—*las doce uvas de la suerte*, our custom. I just had to get through the next two weeks before President-Elect Biden's inauguration, when everything would be quieter. We were planning a family vacation to the Dominican Republic as soon as lockdown restrictions were eased.

At thirty-four, Monica had at last started medical school—her longtime dream—though the pandemic meant she also had to take classes online. Despite being tired from her tough schedule, she made my favorite breakfast: scrambled eggs, Dominican salami, and *mangú*—boiled green plantains smashed with cheese and butter. I wasn't hungry yet, so she packed it up for later, figuring the political brouhaha might make this a long, exhausting day. I kissed my sleeping nine-year-old Emmanuel's forehead whispering, "*Dios bendiga*," and told Monica, "*Te amo*"—I love you—before hopping into my burgundy Jeep Cherokee at 5:30.

On the ride to work, I listened to the podcast *Netflix Is a Joke*. Mexican American comedian Gabriel Iglesias, a.k.a. Mr. Fluffy, riffed about his nineteen-year-old son Frankie who wouldn't leave home or go to college, despite his dad offering to pay for it. He wanted to send his son on an exchange program abroad with a third-world student who'd appreciate basic luxuries American kids took for granted. Laughing, I could relate, thinking how by four years old Emmanuel refused to eat *mangú* with eggs, insisting we make him pancakes and tater tots. Growing up, I'd felt lucky to have enough to eat but never remembered having a choice for breakfast. With my recent raise, I was pleased I could provide my son a better life than I had, though with more responsibility came added stress.

Switching to the local news station, I heard about the violent skirmishes caused by white nationalists protesting in the area. They reported that the chairman of the Proud Boys, Enrique Tarrio, was charged with possessing extended gun magazines when he was arrested for burning a Black Lives Matter banner at a local church. It galled me that his other group, Latinos for Trump, kept backing a candidate who perpetuated racism.

The country felt like it was falling apart. During the tumultuous summer of 2020, a Black protester had yelled right in my face, "You're a pig and a killer!" as I stood next to the bike racks at a D.C. rally. I felt unjustly lumped in with bad guys like Minneapolis cop Derek Chauvin, the man responsible for the death of George Floyd. I was still haunted by that heartbreakingly cruel murder. Watching how helpless Mr. Floyd was on the ground, I told younger officers I worked with, "If you ever see me using excessive force like that, punch me in the face and tackle me so I stop." I couldn't believe Chauvin's bosses had ignored eighteen previous complaints and let him continue as a field training officer.

"What if I called you a thug or gangster, stereotyping you based on your looks, clothes, or skin color?" I asked the protester. "That's what you did to me. You don't know me or my background. If I were there, I would have jumped on Chauvin to stop him from hurting George Floyd."

I was glad he listened as I argued that not everyone in a blue uniform was the same. Too often lately, I'd felt stung by young progressives who defaced the Peace Monument with red spray paint and shouted, "Defund the Police," "Fuck the Police," "Cops are Murderers," and "ACAB," an acronym I looked up that meant "All Cops Are Bastards."

Flipping to Fox News radio, I noted where the next right-wing rallies were planned.

I'd been following the frantic cycle after Trump lost the presidency, fearing the pro–law enforcement Republicans would go against us for just doing our job. I'd heard a bunch of police had recently taken a knee on the East Front of the Capitol in solidarity with BLM protesters. Though we were trained to remain neutral in public, I understood where they were coming from. Many police unions nationwide had endorsed Trump twice, but I hadn't. As he threw paper towels instead of giving food to Puerto Ricans suffering from the devastation of Hurricane Maria, he seemed cold-hearted and lacking in empathy. His racist comments—calling Black nations "shithole countries" and Mexican immigrants "criminals, drug dealers, and rapists"—made me feel targeted and vilified. My son spoke English better than I did. When we traveled, I noticed stares and condescending looks, as if strangers thought I was less American than he was. Or the wrong kind of immigrant. I was outraged that Trump's Slovenian wife came to this country on the kind of visa he suspended, and that she sponsored her parents' citizenship using the "chain migration" he'd denounced to stop nonwhites like my family from moving here. After waiting ten years, three of my uncles still couldn't get visas.

I understood that politics were personal and complicated. I was pro-choice and advocated for vaccines, immigration, gun control, and voting rights for all, but I had relatives I respected who were conservative. Like many families, we agreed to not argue our conflicting viewpoints at dinner. I also tried not to display my beliefs at work, though sometimes I couldn't help it. Like that past November when a coworker said, "Trump wins—unless the election's stolen."

"He's good for my stocks and retirement fund," another supervisor added.

"But not for people of color, with all his racist slurs," I blurted out.

"Oh, he doesn't mean what he says," my coworker insisted, laughing. "People take him too seriously."

"His press secretary just said, 'His tweets speak for themselves,'" I argued.

"Yeah, he does have a big mouth," the supervisor countered. "Most of the time, he's just joking around."

"So when he trashes Blacks and Latinos, that's a funny joke at my expense?" I asked.

The national political divide had infiltrated my workplace. However, I reminded those under my command that we were nonpartisan when it came to protecting everyone equally—even as dissent brewed from the left and right. During the pandemic, Antifa and Black Lives Matter members called us "scum" and "bastards." Conservatives and white supremacists who normally loved cops—giving us thumbs-up signs and yelling "we support you" as we walked by—now labeled us traitors for not allowing interference in election results.

I shut off the radio.

I got to work at 6:10 a.m. I parked in a designated underground garage, closer to the Capitol Grounds than usual. After serving in Iraq, it was usually easy to keep my cool in D.C., but thinking of all my coworkers out sick with COVID and rising right-wing support for overturning the election, I was tense when I clocked in, expecting to have to fill in for all those absent. I checked the weather to see how many layers of clothes I needed. Changing in the locker room, I chose my dark blue mountain bike uniform, more casual than my normal outfit. If I needed my helmet, gas mask, and arm protectors, I'd be sweating—even though it was 40 degrees out. The lighter material was more breathable with heavy gear.

I greeted my staff in the hallway at 7:00 a.m. and briefed them on our schedule. Three different officers showed me #Stopthesteal social media posts that were spurring scuffles nearby. "We're here to protect their First Amendment rights. But we're not their friends," I warned my squad. "If they see us as a barrier to disrupting the exchange of power, it could get out of hand." Awaiting orders, I stayed quiet, checking my cellphone for updates and intel bulletins. Having worked all kinds of protests over the last sixteen years, I was confident we could handle anything.

Still, that week I'd asked my senior sergeant and lieutenant for tabletop training to practice different scenarios and alleviate the palpable concern of my team. I hoped a few question-and-answer sessions would clarify our assignment and quell everyone's anxiety.

"If a protester comes at me, what are the rules?" asked a younger Black officer, a fellow vet.

"If he hits you, he's breaking the law and you can arrest him," the senior sergeant replied.

"If I use force that gets videoed, couldn't I get crucified like Chauvin?" an older white policeman wanted to know.

"Don't murder someone already apprehended and subdued on the ground, Jesus," I jumped in.

"Is a verbal threat an arrestable offense?" a female cop questioned.

"Yes," the lieutenant answered.

"If they say 'Biden lost and Trump won,' isn't that their First Amendment right?" asked an Asian colleague in his twenties.

"Depends if there's a threat attached," the senior sergeant told him.

"What if the threats are online?" he continued. "How do we handle that?"

"Any threats you see, email to me," I told him. "I'll forward them through the chain of command and let you know how to respond."

"Can we deploy our rifles like we did at BLM protests?" the veteran asked. Others agreed they'd feel safer with weapons stronger than our regular handguns. Wanting more protection too, I supported the appeal.

A captain referred our request to the Containment Emergency Response Team (CERT). "As of now you're not authorized to use long guns for the civil disturbances today." He added, "And keep those unruly Black Lives Matter and Antifa protesters away from Trump supporters, so they don't kill each other."

Early that Wednesday morning, none of my bosses seemed to know who our real enemies were or how badly they were about to turn on us.

20

The Thin Blue Line

Washington, D.C., January 6, 2021

A T 7:30 A.M. INSIDE THE CAPITOL POLICE OFFICE, I revised the daily schedule. The coronavirus had severely weakened our force. Dozens were either working remotely or out sick. I covered the vacancies as best as I could with members of my Civil Disturbance Unit. About seventy officers in our division's platoon did roll call together at the Visitor's Center. I was happy to hear Harry Dunn's voice among the group. On any other day, I would have gone over to greet him, but today there was no time. We were fielding a barrage of questions and wearing surgical masks to satisfy pandemic protocol, which added to the anxious atmosphere in the room. After the attendance check, everyone went to the cafeteria to get coffee and carryout.

In the hallway, I saw my colleague Officer Brian Sicknick heading to the break room, wearing his blue mountain bike jacket. He was also a veteran and introvert who was my age. Whenever he worked under my command and I asked him to do overtime or volunteer for anything, he'd jump in and never complain, the type you wanted on your team. We exchanged a brief hello.

Back at my desk, I ate the meal Monica had prepared for me, listening to reggaeton on my cell phone while waiting for updates from my police radio. The peaceful moment was brief. A few members of my unit soon interrupted to share disturbing Twitter, Facebook, and Instagram posts spreading election misinformation and vague threats we couldn't corroborate.

At 8:17 a.m. Trump had just posted an unnerving tweet: "States want to correct their votes, which they now know were based on irregularities and fraud, plus corrupt process . . . All Mike Pence has to do is send them back to the States, AND WE WIN. Do it Mike, this is a time for extreme courage!"

It was disconcerting to watch clips of Trump speaking to his supporters at a rally near the White House. "WE WILL NEVER GIVE UP. WE WILL NEVER CONCEDE!" He ended his rant by commanding his supporters to march to the Capitol "TO TAKE BACK OUR COUNTRY."

Videos of Republican senators being swarmed by Trump fans on the Hill were circulating. In one, Rudy Giuliani stood behind a SAVE AMERICA sign and further incited the crowd. I shook my head in disgust as he said, "It seems to me, we don't want to find out three weeks from now even more proof that this election was stolen, do we? . . . Let's have trial by combat."

I found Trump and Giuliani's rhetoric agitating, but from my desk at work, at least, the next few hours proceeded in a normal fashion. The Senate was set to convene to count the electoral votes and confirm Joe Biden as the winner of the 2020 election around noon. My squad was instructed to use the same procedures we had used for other demonstrations in the past. No change of protocol was ordered, nor did the gathering demonstrations trigger the kind of urgency we'd seen during BLM protests. Yet the enraged right-wing social media pictures and quotes I kept seeing were surreal, like they were coming from another country. They revealed a different story that was much more distressing than the intel I was getting from my superiors.

Around 11:00 a.m., both House and Senate Sergeants at Arms requested additional officers for inside posts to prevent interruptions during the transfer of power. I and other supervisors pushed back, explaining we didn't have anyone else to spare but the CDU platoons on standby in case something happened. Their response was "make it happen." When we did, we lost a dozen officers.

Around 12:50 p.m., the call came. My radio blared, "All CDU officers to the West Front! Send all you have!"

It sounded like an emergency.

"Hurry. Get your gear," I told my Civil Disturbance team. "Help each other out."

After putting on chest, arm, and thigh protectors and my helmet, I grabbed my utility belt with extra ammo, radio, pepper spray, handcuffs, shield, and collapsible baton. Everyone followed suit. There were reports on the radio of pipe bombs found at both the Republican National Committee and the Democratic National Committee buildings (Vice President-Elect Harris was in a holding room in the latter). But live-streaming news on social media was filling us in on the developing situation more than government officials were.

I led a few dozen members of my unit from the North Visitor Center to the West Front. I opened the heavy double doors leading to Emancipation Hall. Rushing through the underground steps, we ran the equivalent of a block to the Crypt and down another hallway to where I'd seen Presidents Bush and Obama sworn in.

About 1:00 p.m., we neared the Lower West Terrace entrance. I was already sweaty and uncomfortable, but as we came closer, my heartbeat raced. Just beyond the doors, the surging crowd roared. I was blindsided by the magnitude of the violence.

An angry mob of rioters swirled around the inaugural stage,

shouting and fighting the police already on the scene. I didn't yet know that my Capitol colleague Caroline Edwards had already suffered a concussion at Peace Circle on the other side of the West Front.

The back of my eyes went hot as I witnessed my fellow officers brazenly beaten with pipes, sticks, and rocks by rioters chanting "Fight for Trump" and "USA! USA!" Trump banners outnumbered American flags, and for a second I froze in fear. I'd seen this kind of unbridled rage in Iraq when the base had been under attack, and I knew this was bad. We were surrounded on all sides, yet there wasn't time to coordinate. At the academy, we'd been taught how to create a tactical barrier. My training kicked in. Without a thought, we leapt into the fray to help our comrades hold the police line, maneuvering beside them in a row to show solidarity. Holding the line was the way to stand our ground and keep the invaders at bay.

An onslaught of rioters jumped us. My officers were getting hit, punched, and stabbed with broken-off parts of a bike rack and anything else the rioters could find.

"Get back! Get back!" I yelled.

I kept my shield in front of me to fight off a swarm of attackers. An old white guy with a beard jabbed at me with a pole from the side, near my groin and thighs. I fended off another bearded nut, this one in a military helmet and blue jacket as he tried to wrestle my baton and portable radio cord away. As pepper spray came at my face, I donned my gas mask. My gloves were slippery from the sprayed chemicals, so I took them off. Trained officers hurled stun grenades and pepper-ball ammo at the agitators from the top of the inaugural stage. A round hit a Trump supporter in the cheek, his blood gushing. Two of us went to assist him, causing another agitator to go berserk, thinking we were arresting him.

"Why are you attacking him for no reason?" he yelled.

For no reason? This was the most ruthless rampage I'd ever witnessed. Many of these barbarians were armed, so we refrained from using lethal force, afraid of provoking a massacre. Some of the rioters seemed disorderly and chaotic, but they were dangerous and the situation was deteriorating fast. We were losing ground to the madness. The thought that we couldn't hold our police queue petrified me. We didn't have enough backup to control the relentless havoc.

Someone threw an American flag on the floor and screamed "Pick it up!" as a kind of inverted rally cry. I was stunned that they desecrated the sacred symbol of our country and blamed it on us, to further incite their furious hordes. I asked a coworker to pick it up and he did. It pacified the rioters, but not for long. An officer next to me was tackled to the ground by a blond guy in a camouflage jacket. As I went to grab the aggressor, a different rioter in a burgundy hoodie attacked me with a stolen police baton. He smashed my hand. The pain was excruciating.

At 1:05 p.m. Vice President Mike Pence issued a statement: "My oath to support and defend the Constitution constrains me from claiming unilateral authority to determine which electoral votes should be counted and which should not." It was retweeted with a vengeance as Speaker of the House Nancy Pelosi banged the gavel to call the joint session of Congress to order to confirm Joe Biden as president. By 1:08 p.m. a wave of enraged, irrational protesters stormed the outer police barrier on the East Front, screaming, "Hang Mike Pence!"

I couldn't see it at the time, but at 1:30 p.m., the burgeoning mob overcame the police stationed outside the Capitol's east side. Breaching the barricades, they pushed inside and threw doors open for their fellow rioters. The House and Senate proceeded without knowledge of the insurgents encircling the building from all sides.

Senate Majority Leader Mitch McConnell took the floor and declared that "voters, the courts, and the states have all spoken . . . If we overrule them, it would damage our republic forever." Immediately following his statement, lawmakers went into lockdown.

"All buildings within the Capitol Complex: External security threat, no entry or exit is permitted, stay away from exterior windows, doors. If outside, seek cover" was the message emailed and texted to cell phones from my command center. I later learned that Capitol Police officer Eugene Goodman—who I'd worked with for years—escorted Senator Mitt Romney to safety. Goodman was able to divert protesters from the Senate's chamber, saving our elected officials from a very close call.

Around 2:00 p.m., Metropolitan Police Mountain Bike Units marched down the inaugural steps in their yellow-and-black jackets and white helmets. The flush of relief I felt upon seeing them faded fast. Only a few dozen reinforcements were on hand to combat a streaming crowd of tens of thousands of rioters.

Perched at the Lower West Front Terrace of the Capitol Building, all I knew was that we were fucked. I took a breath. I couldn't catch much air. My asthma was returning with a vengeance. My chest was tight, making it impossible to breathe. My body was shaking. The adrenaline was keeping me focused, and my training had protected me, but nothing could change the fact that our insufficient manpower left us at a total disadvantage against the deluge. We had an active invasion. The Capitol Building was being breached by armed insurgents! *Where was the military? The FBI? Homeland Security? Why the fuck hadn't the president sent in the National Guard?*

Just six months earlier, I'd worked a local Black Lives Matter and Antifa demonstration filled with a diverse array of mostly unarmed protesters. Nineteen federal agencies had been called in for protection. Armored vehicles had patrolled the city and police helicopters hovered above. Various branches of the military, the National Guard, the Secret Service, the Bureau of Prisons, the U.S. Marshals, and other government agents erected roadblocks, deployed tear gas, and discharged rubber bullets. I was one of thousands of uniformed policemen on site with loaded weapons ready to use. We were shoulder to shoulder, tripping over each other. Police commanders told us the show of force would scare off the BLM demonstrators—mainly Democrats, mostly people of color—to keep them from causing trouble.

"This is an overwhelming show of manpower," I'd told my supervisor, Marvin Reid, a bespectacled Black lieutenant in his fifties who was my height, five foot seven.

"It's crazy. They are really overdoing it," he agreed. "But this is what the higher-ups ordered."

It didn't seem like a coincidence that most of the higher-ups in Trump's administration were white.

Seeing all the guys on high alert in military fatigues reminded me of being on a convoy in Iraq. I admitted as much to Lieutenant Reid. "It's triggering my PTSD."

"Go inside and come back when you're feeling better," he said. "Take the time you need."

I'd drunk a bottle of water before returning to resume supervising the plethora of combat-ready officers standing in unbreakable lines to disperse the BLM protesters on the West Front of the Capitol.

Now, on January 6, only about four hundred members of my CDU-trained force were on site to fight off more than a hundred times the number of rioters on all sides of the Capitol. The federal government could mobilize to aid international hurricanes and tsunamis within hours, but they weren't protecting their own defense forces sixteen blocks from the White House. Recalling Trump's incendiary speech earlier, I had the horrifying realization that nobody else would help us today. Trump wasn't shutting down this dangerous free-for-all because he wanted it. They were doing this on his behalf. His constituents and fans—95 percent white, many armed and dangerous—had heeded his call to come here and fight for him, to keep him in power. He'd told them to do this. We'd all heard it. The Republicans in power weren't anywhere near as terrified of the white nationalists breaching the Capitol as they'd been of left-wing protesters. In fact, right-wing politicians had abetted the mob. Those authorizing reinforcements were appointed by Trump and either took his side or didn't want to upset him. Because of that bootlicking and flagrant dereliction of duty, my troops were exposed, vulnerable, and out in the cold. We were abandoned.

To stop the mayhem, we defended ourselves with fire extinguishers, our collapsible batons, and sprinklers. The air filled with smoke from pepper rounds and pesticides. They hurled bear sprays and full cans of soda at us, making pipes and a giant Trump banner with a metal frame into ramming devices, weakening our queue. This was worse than Iraq.

Broken bike racks used as projectiles were shot our way, forcing us to retreat to the southwest corner of the stage. Since no rescuers were coming, we tried to get control ourselves. But we were tired and beaten; we couldn't contain the waves of assault and walked backward. A tall white guy erected a wooden board from the stage that he used as a big shield as three other guys sprayed chemicals at me. Out of the corner of my eye, I saw a Black guy in an olive green hoodie swing a pole at me so hard it broke my shield. I braced myself near a bloody ledge. There was only one way to go, up.

Pushing through feelings of claustrophobia, I struggled my way up the stairs through the smoke to regroup with other police. At the top of the stage, a Metropolitan Police official screamed, "Get inside!" As the crowd shoved forward, I walked backward through the iconic tunnel where I'd once protected Presidents Bush and Obama as they walked out to be sworn in. I heard glass shatter.

"They broke the door! They're coming in!" someone warned.

I was heartened to hear Police Deputy Commander Ramey J. Kyle yell, "Hold the line! They're not fucking taking the Capitol!" He looked my age and height but had the presence of General Patton mobilizing troops in World War II.

A call went out. "Shields to the front!"

With three members of my squad, I mustered the energy to move to the front of the line, face-to-face with the mob. We kept forcing everyone out of the tunnel. Because Officer Devan Gowdy had written his name on the chest of his gear, the crowd taunted him, screaming out "Gowdy, Gowdy is scared," grabbing his shield, and slamming his face. I saw him fall, but as I was being attacked myself, I couldn't get to him. I later learned he was taken to the hospital with a concussion.

With no idea of the seriousness of my injuries, I returned to the middle of the melee. A man with long hair threw a speaker from the stage at us. He mistakenly hit another rioter in the back of the head, drawing blood. The thick metal box then bounced off him and crashed down on me, smashing my right foot. With my toes and hand wounded I could barely move, but I teetered forward.

"Help me. I can't breathe," screamed a young blond woman with a nose ring and Redskins football hat who was stampeded before me inside the tunnel. It was impossible to reason with the crowd. "Stop. Let her leave." Trying to assist, I was doused by the fire sprinklers and chemicals. The open wounds on my skin were burning. Looking down, I was shocked to see my blood-streaked shield and both of my hands bleeding.

"You are *not* getting through," I told her, trying to ignore my burning hand.

She left but then came right back.

"Didn't you just tell me you couldn't breathe?" I asked. Her duplicity was staggering.

She ignored me. "Keep pushing," she told her fellow rioters.

Next to her, Metropolitan Police officer Daniel Hodges was getting stomped on. He was trapped between the mob, other officers, and the door frame. Hodges's agonizing shrieks haunted me. Getting trampled two rows behind him, I couldn't do anything. My lungs were tightening. I was wheezing. Exhausted, bleeding, my limbs battered, it felt like this was it. My phone vibrated. I knew Monica was calling, but I couldn't answer or move. Lacking oxygen, I was scared I wouldn't get out of there alive, and I resigned myself to it. At least I'd said *"Te amo"* to her that morning before I left and had blessed my little boy.

21

Law and Disorder

Washington, D.C., January 6, 2021

WITH THE SHIELD OF MY GAS MASK CLOUDY FROM my heavy breathing, I couldn't see. Opening my elbows expanded my lungs so I could take in air. Pulled forward, continuing to fend off everyone who wasn't in blue, I worried about the men and women in my unit struggling with me, praying they'd survive.

A slim gray-haired man in a black jacket was acting like a tunnel commander, pushing the mob to work in unison. I subsequently recognized him as the Ohio right-wing extremist David Mehaffie. He was caught on film issuing orders with hand signals, creating waves of reinforcement troops, one wrathful group of amateur militia replaced with fresh agitators. A guy in an orange hat bellowed, "Trump sent us!" At that moment I knew just how premeditated this all was. It was not simply a protest getting out of hand. This was a conspiracy of right-wing extremists battling with a clear mission to seize the Capitol. Online sleuths wound up identifying the armed militia in the crowd as members of the Proud Boys, Oath Keepers, This Is Texas Freedom Force, and neo-Nazis, not that hard to do since they'd videotaped themselves committing the crimes. Several admitted that they'd interpreted Trump's tweet to his supporters in December—"Big protest in D.C. on January 6th. Be there, will be wild!"—as a call to arms.

Yet all I could see at that second was my team—in full riot gear—with a group of D.C. Metropolitan Police. We kept shoving back the charging mob and they kept chanting their inflammatory slogans: "Fight for Trump!" "Stop protecting Congress!" "Stop the steal!" "We're doing this for you!" "If Biden's elected, it'll be like living in China!"

Insanity, every last word.

In the building where I'd first contemplated the profound carnage and rage of the Civil War and America's cruel legacy of racism, I was now enmeshed in a brutal siege that went on for more than four hours, my team jabbed, punched, and blinded with lasers by savages wielding guns, hammers, knives, and a flagpole.

The entrance floor was slippery with blood, vomit, and pepper spray and one of the MPD officers fell while shoving back the crowd. Fear flashed in his eyes but I couldn't get to him because a rioter with a red beard and white butcher coat pulled me hard by my arm strap. He refused to let go, like he was tearing my limb from my shoulder blade. I feared I'd be dragged into the crowd. I thought of grabbing my gun to use deadly force, knowing it would be justified. But after I got in a blow, another MPD officer hit the butcher and other rioters fell on top of him, loosening his grip on me.

"Help me, pull me the fuck back up," I hollered. My left shoulder throbbed. I was terrified nobody could hear me through my gas mask, with all the shouting and fire alarms going off. I backpedaled and grabbed the rail to push myself up and struggled to the rear of the police line to call for more backup.

Inside the Rotunda, members of Congress posted pictures of themselves putting masks on to protect themselves from tear gas. Soon after, rioters swarmed the Senate chambers. They jumped from the balcony, climbed on podiums to take selfies, and marched through the Capitol. They stormed Pelosi's office, chanting, "Break it down, break it down." They punched the doorway's glass panels, creating extensive damage, and screamed, "Fuck the blue!"

A man in a MAKE AMERICA GREAT AGAIN hoodie told an officer, "When the whole country hated you, we had your back."

There were loud shrieks at 2:40 p.m. as a policeman with a gun took over guarding the door to the Speaker's Lobby outside the House chambers. In the videos I saw afterward, thirty-five-year-old rioter and air force veteran Ashli Babbitt, draped in a Trump flag as a cape, angrily demanded officers step aside. The officers held the line, but Babbitt wasn't deterred. Assisted by two men, she began to climb through a section of the broken doors. She ignored commands to stop. In an attempt to protect the elected officials still in the House Chamber, Lieutenant Michael Byrd fired off a shot that hit her neck and sent her tumbling back into the crowd. Officers rushed to help Babbitt, who had bypassed and breached multiple layers of security, ignoring officers giving her commands to stop. She was transported to Washington Hospital Center, where she later died. Reports indicated a fifty-five-year-old Alabama protester had dropped dead of a heart attack on the west side of the building. I heard of other deaths and injuries but couldn't confirm any while standing my ground.

Around 3:15, a second group of Metropolitan Police moved in. I had to relieve myself badly, so I didn't hesitate when a tall white officer with a mask covering his face offered to take my spot. This was Michael Fanone, though at that point, I didn't know his name.

"Let's get some fresh guys," he said, replacing me on the front line.

On my way to the bathroom, Representatives Annie Kuster and Veronica Escobar passed by with their staffs, who were being rushed to secure rooms yards away from the fighting.

I forgot to rinse the chemicals off my hands before using the urinal.

A searing pain burned through my groin. When it passed, I washed my hands with soap and rushed back to my colleagues.

White smoke wafted through the air as I returned to find Fanone being dragged on the ground by rioters who'd grabbed his Glock. "Kill him with his own gun," they shouted. Other MPD officers quickly intervened, surrounding Fanone and carrying him and his weapon through the tunnel to safety. Just before I'd come back, he'd been tased in the back of the neck, suffering a heart attack and traumatic brain injury. In Iraq, when Sergeant Prendergast let the three soldiers go ahead in the PX line, I'd narrowly avoided catastrophe. The only difference today was that Officer Fanone's fearlessness saved me, not random chance.

Yet in the scuffle, I was pushed down. I grabbed a guardrail to regain my balance, slipping once more before managing to pull myself to the rear of the police line. Coughing, aching, and unable to breathe, I threw off my helmet and gas mask and inhaled deeply to get some air in and calm down. I found paper towels on a supply cart and wiped off the helmet shield as best I could. Then I grabbed some bottles of water and distributed them to comrades in worse shape than I was as I returned to the front lines.

While other officers left that entrance due to injuries or exhaustion, I stayed. Pushing forward to the mouth of Lower West Terrace entrance a little after 4:00 p.m., my eyes were blinded by chemicals as blows from insurrectionists kept raining down on me. I put my gas mask on again.

I didn't know it yet, but Trump had further incited the mob with a series of tweets, turning them against the vice president by claiming that "Mike Pence didn't have the courage to do what should have been done to protect our Country and our Constitution." Looking back, that's around when I got my shoulder injured. The mob became more violent, seeming to follow his orders.

At 4:17, Trump posted video messages instructing the violent mob to leave the Capitol. "Go home," he said, adding, "We love you, you're very special." They didn't listen. By the time he was finally compelled to tell his people to "stay peaceful," it was too late. I was badly injured and the fighting was still raging. Rioters I'd seen at the police line earlier returned for a second crack at entering where I was. Some I later recognized on videos, breaching other entrances since they couldn't get through the tunnel. The National Guard was supposedly deployed by 4:30, but all I saw was rioters still punching and pulling me, further damaging my shoulder as my leg twisted in agony.

Inside the tunnel, behind its ballistic podium, I watched several officers carrying a young protester who'd collapsed to safety. "Request medical assistance and D.C. Fire!" I yelled as someone checked her vitals. No response. An officer did compressions on her chest to resuscitate her as firecrackers landed nearby. A guy in a MAGA hat attempted to blind us with eye-damaging lasers as we desperately tried to save the rioter.

"Sarge, D.C. Fire can't respond because the area isn't secure," someone on my team rushed over to tell me. "They're afraid to come without an escort."

We didn't have any free officers to escort firefighters anywhere; we needed help holding the line and getting our own wounded to safety. After moving her behind a wall, I went inside the hallway and grabbed two defibrillators. A coworker hurried to shock her body back to life, but the wires connecting the pad to the first yellow machine broke. Before we could pull out the second one, three agents in olive fatigues rushed up, carrying a camouflaged medical bag.

"Make way. I'm a medic with the FBI," said the one taking over, putting a tube in her throat to help her breathe. We administered CPR again. No pulse. A flagpole landed next to us, then a hammer. White smoke from fire extinguishers and pepper spray stained the air. The mob kept attacking even while we tended to their wounded.

"Move her. It's not safe here," I screamed over the noise.

We put her on a black military two-wheeled gurney that six of us carried up two flights to the Crypt, since the elevators were in evacuation mode. We thought it would be safer there. Using my bruised left arm to lift her, I grabbed the handrails with my right hand to pull myself up. The cop next to me almost dropped her. A tall guy rushed down to replace him, saying "I got you." I was pleased it was Harry Dunn, who I hadn't seen since roll call early that morning.

As we moved her up the stairs, dust and debris flew everywhere. My injured officers were throwing up, coughing, bleeding, and tending to their injuries.

"What happened up here?" I asked Harry. At this moment, I'd still assumed the protesters had only stormed the Lower West Terrace where I was. I had no idea they'd infiltrated all the Capitol entrances.

"We tried to push them back, but the crowd broke through," Harry told me.

"From where?" I asked as we took her down the ramp past House Majority Leader Steny Hoyer's office, where it seemed less perilous. "We didn't let anybody in."

"They broke windows and doors from the other sides." Harry shook his head in dismay. "They got in from everywhere."

Because we'd held the rioters back at the tunnel, senators and members of Congress were able to make it to their secured hideaways, but I was devastated to learn the full scope of the invasion.

We found an empty spot to lay the tattooed woman down and continued CPR for an hour, switching off between FBI medic and my team. We couldn't save her. We waited for the D.C. ambulance to arrive to take her to the hospital, where she was pronounced dead. We didn't even know her name. Her ID was lost in the tunnel. Any other day, faster treatment would have given her a better chance for survival.

The south doors were closed and quarantined. Police tape marked it as a crime scene. "What happened down there?" I asked an officer.

"A shooting," he said. "A female was killed when she tried to break into the House chambers. She fought past eight layers of security."

This was the first I'd heard about the death of Ashli Babbitt. After protesters pulled on the cord of my portable police radio, almost choking me with it, I'd let it dangle off the side of my hip. I'd been too frazzled to check for updates.

Finding a quiet spot away from the fray, I listened to the flurry of messages Monica had left. "I'm watching the news, worried about you. Are you okay? Everyone's calling: my parents, your mom, dad, brothers, sister, Grandpa Bienvenido and Grandma Andrea, and Sergeant Prendergast from Coney Island. We love you. May God protect you."

"I'm okay," I texted her back, unsure if I was. "Love you."

BACK AT THE Lower West Terrace entrance nearing 5:30, I was beyond relieved to find the National Guard had intervened to disperse the crowd with overwhelming force and flashbangs. The agitators were pushed out of the Capitol Grounds onto Peace Circle and the streets. The melee had stopped, but the whole area reeked of so much smoke and toxic spray that the newly arrived replacements were coughing.

"Put your masks on," I called out.

At the inaugural stage, I texted the acting sergeant to find out if everyone in my squad had survived and where they were. Most were gathered at the Law Library door near the Old Supreme Court, sitting outside on the winding staircase to catch their breath after four hours of bloodshed. By the Crypt, my team was bruised and beaten, crying, consoling each other. Everybody made it out alive, but three had concussions. Another was in the ER with a dislocated shoulder, twisted neck, and broken finger. Numb and in shock, I didn't report my injuries.

"Anyone need medical assistance?" I asked.

"No, Sarge." They were also playing down how badly they'd been injured.

"Go grab something to eat. Use the bathroom. Call your family and let them know you survived. But keep listening to the radio in case more insurgents turn up and we're needed," I warned.

I remained on high alert. Intelligence updates on my email warned that white supremacists were returning to the Capitol, this time with firearms. Lawmakers weren't cleared to return to finish tallying the electoral votes until 8:00 p.m. that night, and they wouldn't be released until the certification of the transfer of presidential power was completed.

Taking the stairs down to the Detail Office, I marched up to my captain's desk and tore into him. "Why didn't we have more reinforcements? We could have all died out there!"

"The whole Capitol was breached," he responded. "We were surprised and completely overwhelmed on all sides!"

While battered members of my unit rested on couches, benches, and floors of the break room and hallway, I couldn't relax or let my guard down. I obsessed over news updates. Mitch McConnell, Kevin McCarthy, Nancy Pelosi, Mike Pence, and everybody on both chamber floors knew Trump incited the riots and said so. It made the subsequent denials by Republicans more infuriating.

A radio dispatch told us to decontaminate our equipment, so I took my gear to the janitor's storage closet and rinsed off the blood and chemicals as best I could. Wanting to be useful, I put on my mountain bike jacket and returned to the Lower West Terrace entrance to find the ID of the tattooed woman we couldn't revive, hoping to alert her family before they heard her fate on the news. I waded through weapons on the ground, broken police shields, flagpoles, speakers, broken glass, empty water bottles, a sledgehammer, and ripped MAGA hats and T-shirts. At the bottom of the stage area where the battle had taken place, I snapped pictures of the destruction with my work phone as proof while FBI agents and crime scene investigators collected and tagged evidence.

"What are you doing here?" a CSI asked.

"I'm Sergeant Gonell. I was fighting here earlier today." I showed my ID, explaining what I was looking for.

On the ground, I saw something by a surgical mask. Under a scarf with a MAGA 2020 logo and a white Trump cowboy hat, I found a loose driver's license covered in muck. I recognized the picture. She was a thirty-four-year-old woman from Georgia named Rosanne Boyland. We assumed she died from being trampled by the crowd, though the D.C. Medical Examiner wound up ruling the cause of death to be "accidental acute amphetamine intoxication," a drug overdose.

"I'm pretty sure this is the woman we gave CPR, but she didn't make it," I told the investigator. I took a picture of the ID before handing it over.

"Where did you find it?" she asked. I pointed to the entrance of the arch.

Monica sent several more anxious texts and voice mails. I called her back. She wanted to know if I was okay and when I would be home.

"Don't know, baby, dealing with security stuff." I didn't tell her about the dead woman. Or my asthma flare-up, throbbing shoulder, or hand and foot problems. "Give Manny a hug for me." My voice cracked. I took a breath to not lose it and scare her. "Try to get some sleep."

"I can't. I'll have dinner waiting for you," she said.

The hours of fending off crazed invaders caught up with me and I broke down, sweating, dizzy, hands shaking. Hearing someone coming, I gathered myself and checked my phone for updates on security changes. Back at my desk at the Detail Office at 10:00 p.m., adrenal glands still pumped up and unable to calm down, I robotically redid the schedule for the next day, removing officers who were hurt or hospitalized. I sent the updated list through the chain of command.

"Will you have your injuries looked at by the medical staff?" Lieutenant Reid asked.

"It's okay. I'm good to go," I said, shoring up my energy to stay in control, nowhere near ready to come out of denial.

"Where are you?" Monica texted again.

"Home soon," I replied.

Over the radio my supervisor told us we could go home at 3:00 a.m. after reinforcements from multiple agencies took over.

"Brian Sicknick was taken to the hospital after collapsing in the office," I heard someone say.

"What happened to Brian?" I asked, alarmed.

"He got hit and sprayed," the officer told me. "We called the ambulance and took him to the Senate door. He's in critical condition."

On the Senate floor, Republican Senators Ted Cruz and Josh Hawley were objecting to certifying the electoral votes—even after the attacks, they were still echoing President Trump's false claims that the election he lost was stolen.

"I can't believe this horror show," I said, shaking my head.

Congress declared Joe Biden the winner of the 2020 presidential election at 3:41 a.m.

"We just got word they'll let us go." I called Monica from my office phone as a mad dash of officers left. "This all happened because one rich white spoiled seventy-four-year-old racist was a sore loser." It freaked me out that 74 million Americans had voted for Trump and that right-wing politicians were already rationalizing away the desecration he'd just caused. It had almost killed me.

"Just get home, baby," Monica pleaded.

I limped to my car, half in stupor. I was in the same uniform I'd fought in, carrying my backpack and lunch bag, and thinking how close I came to not making it home.

"On my way," I let Monica know from the drive, after I recharged my cell phone.

"Thank god," she said. "What's going on there now?"

I was too out of it to respond. "Tell you when I get home."

I turned on salsa music to take my mind off of how I'd barely survived.

I parked in my driveway and at 4:00 a.m. walked slowly up the porch, my limp getting worse. Monica was waiting for me. I wanted to wrap my arms around her, but when she reached out, I put my hand out to stop her. "Don't touch me," I cautioned. "I have noxious spray all over my body."

"What do you need? How can I help?"

"Bring Clorox wipes."

Inside, I dropped my bag in the corner and took off my shoes, pants, utility belt, gun, and bulletproof vest. She tried to help me take off my shirt. "Don't," I said, keeping my mask on. "Be careful." I walked down the steps to the laundry room naked, put my clothes in the washer, then took a shower. But the water only reactivated the cocktail of chemicals on my burning skin.

"Help, bring me milk!" I called out, thinking it would neutralize the chemicals.

I poured the carton over myself, but it didn't stop the stinging.

"Here, try these," she said, returning with bottles of moisturizer and lotion.

I tried each brand, but it didn't soothe the inflammation. If anything, the moisture only worsened it.

I took another shower but couldn't wash the day off me.

Wrapping a sheet around myself, I finally held Monica and sobbed for ten minutes, unable to process what I'd been through. Drying myself lightly with towels, I saw bruises on my left shoulder, legs, foot, and all over my lower body. I wanted to lie down, but I couldn't move or turn. Even my cotton basketball shorts irritated my skin; everything did.

Upstairs in the kitchen, Monica had put out chicken noodle soup, rice, beans, and Caesar salad with a glass of mango juice.

"Why did you make so much food?"

"I couldn't sleep. I need to keep busy."

I drank the soup and juice, but I had no appetite and was uncomfortable sitting down.

"Eat a little more," she pushed, so I took a few bites of rice.

"How could this happen in the United States?" I asked. "This shit happens where we come from. And in third world countries. Not here. I almost died waiting for the fucking president to send in the National Guard while he's watching it all go down on TV at the White House, two miles away."

She came over to hug me. I let her, ignoring my throbbing shoulder and foot. Noticing my hand was bleeding, she said "Let's go to the emergency room. I'll get someone to watch Manny."

"No, I'm okay," I kept repeating, to convince myself.

I peeked in my son's room. He was sleeping soundly. In case I'd caught COVID during the hand-to-hand combat with thousands of rioters not wearing masks, I decided to sleep in the basement so I wouldn't expose Monica or Manny.

WAKING UP AT 7:00 a.m. the next morning, I went upstairs to see Monica was already up.

"Are you going to the hospital now?" she asked.

"No, I have to work. My team's ordered back at 9:00 a.m." As their sergeant, I had to be there an hour early.

"That's ridiculous, after what you've been through," she said.

My son was still asleep. Putting on a face mask, I went to his room to bless him before I left.

Hardly able to walk or move my arm, I couldn't even open the refrigerator door to get water. I told myself I was lucky I hadn't lost my life. Yet over the last twenty-four hours, I'd lost my health, hope, sense of equilibrium, and faith in this country. Everything I'd fought so hard for was disintegrating and I couldn't stop it.

22

Detail Office

Washington, D.C., January 7, 2021

"How you feeling, Aqueano?" asked Lieutenant Reid.

"I can't believe after three years you still can't get it right, Marvin!" He wasn't the only boss to mispronounce my name; my fellow midnight sergeant had taken to calling me "Go Go."

"Gonell, you get any sleep?" Reid said instead of asking how to say it and trying again.

"Barely two hours," I admitted.

On the back end of my eighteen-hour shift on Thursday, January 7, he'd requested a typed report updating the injury status of the officers on my team.

Reid noticed my swollen hands and bleeding knuckles. "Better get yourself checked out."

"I'm okay. I can still fire from my shooting hand if I need to," I told him, though I couldn't get a firm grip on anything. I insisted my officers go to the on-site medical team. As a military sergeant, my troops were my priority. Good leaders found shelter, grabbed a blanket, or ate after everyone else. I was supposed to be the first to come and last to leave. I carried that mentality to the police force.

"Dude, get it checked out," he pushed. He was the only boss to express concern for my health.

Now that the disaster was over and we didn't need reinforcements, 20,000 active National Guard troops were everywhere. They helped us replace lost equipment, patrol the area, and check identification to make sure all those present were authorized to be there. Thousands of mostly white assailants broke the law by breaching the Capitol the day before, but already the buildings had been thoroughly washed, mopped, and fumigated by a mostly Black maintenance crew. It bothered me that it had already reopened. Given the magnitude of what had happened, the Capitol complex should have remained a restricted crime scene. I'd even turned in my broken shield, assuming it would serve as evidence.

At 8:00 p.m., a captain gathered us at Emancipation Hall in the Visitor Center. "Officer Sicknick is in a coma," he announced. "The news incorrectly reported that a Capitol Police officer died, but he hasn't. Do not post this information on social media or share with anyone."

I tried not to tear up in front of everyone. "If you're religious, please pray for Brian. And remain vigilant in case these rioters return," I told my team. From an officer who'd assisted Sicknick, I learned he'd collapsed in the Detail Office where they'd given him CPR and wheelchaired him to the ambulance at the Senate door.

AN INTERNAL BULLETIN showed a new protest announced for the next day. We were deployed in full CDU gear to the top of the Upper

D House office garage for three hours, but only five unarmed protesters showed up. They called us "traitors who supported tyranny" and chanted "Trump 2020." Despite the small scale of the demonstration, I was tense and on edge. It reminded me of Iraq, when I never knew when or where the bombs would go off.

Feeling worse Friday, I decided to see a doctor. I warned my bosses I'd be late. I went to a medical center where I'd once been treated for a basketball injury. Since I'd be heading to work later, I wore my uniform, asking for the doctor who'd seen me in the past.

"She's not in today. I can set up an appointment when she's available," the receptionist offered.

"I'll see someone else. I'm badly hurt. It's an emergency." Saying those words out loud made me feel weaker, like I was about to fall apart again.

"Let me check if Dr. Hampton is available," she said.

"Tell him I'm a police officer injured during the riots at the Capitol." I mustered my nerve, flashing back to the violence coming at me from all sides, reliving each blow. The room, crowded with patients and medical staff, went quiet. I was paranoid they were staring at me. It was my job to be strong.

"Can I go to the back?" I asked, embarrassed to lose it in front of everyone.

In a corner room, a tall, skinny white orthopedic surgeon about my age introduced himself as Dr. Hampton. "What happened?" he asked. "What can I do for you?"

"Defending the Capitol Wednesday, I almost got killed by rioters," I managed to gasp out, sobbing. "They smashed my foot, shoulder, and hands." I showed him the bruises and lacerations all over my body.

"I saw the news. You're lucky you survived. I can't imagine what you've been through," he said, examining me gently. "Let's get you X-rays and a shoulder MRI. And one for your foot and right thumb.

You need a specialist. There's serious damage here. I'm putting you on restricted duty."

"No, don't. We just got attacked. I need to help my team implement new security at the Capitol. I can come back on January 21, right after Biden's inauguration."

"If that's what you want, I won't fight you," Dr. Hampton said. "But I don't recommend it."

At 1:00 p.m., a few hours after I walked into the office, a supervisor said, "You need to go home."

"Why?" I asked. Had he heard about my doctor visit?

"An officer fighting next to you in the tunnel Wednesday just tested positive," he explained. "You should isolate in case you were exposed."

"I was wearing my mask the whole time," I argued. "I have no symptoms."

"Not my call," he said. "Go get tested."

I called Monica at home, interrupting her online microbiology class, for help to find a nearby urgent care that did COVID-19 testing. But the results wouldn't come in until Saturday.

"Stay with Manny on the main floor and I'll sleep downstairs until I get my test back," I FaceTimed Monica on my way home.

We both had masks on, but I kept my distance when I got to the house. Monica had packed some pizza and chicken wings into my lunchbox. I took it downstairs to eat alone.

"Manny's here, he wants to say hi," she FaceTimed to say.

"*Hola, Papi*," said my nine-year-old, staring at me from the small screen. "Are you okay? How are you feeling? I saw what happened on TV. How come those people attacked the Capitol?"

"I'm okay. I don't know why they did that." I lied to shield him.

"Will you get better so we can play basketball?"

"Soon," I promised. "I owe you a big hug and kiss."

The results from my medical exams soon detailed how bad the damage was: contusion of the left shoulder; contusion of the right hand; contusion of the right foot; strained muscle and tendonitis on lower left leg; dislocation of right toe on right foot requiring bone fusion; metatarsalgia of right foot; rotator cuff and labrum tear; bicep damage; right thumb cyst; lacerations on hand, arm, and groin area; ocular pain; chronic PTSD reactivated. Dr. Hampton scheduled me for a more comprehensive evaluation with other specialists.

That night CNN announced Sicknick's death, caused by two strokes he'd had a day after fighting back the attackers. Gone at forty-two. My age, also born the end of July, Brian was a fellow veteran who'd served overseas, with the New Jersey Air National Guard. "Turn on CNN. Brian Sicknick died," I texted Monica, devastated. "That could have been me."

"I know, I just saw footage of the attack on TV and knew it was you because I recognized your hand raised with your crooked pinkie. You were right in the middle of it," she texted back. "Thank god you're safe and here with us now." She added a heart emoji.

During a commercial, I flipped the channel. I landed on Fox News, where a host claimed that the protests were started by Antifa and that police let the rioters in voluntarily. I wanted to scream. People had died and 140 officers were incapacitated, suffering from brain swelling, cracked ribs, smashed spinal disks, stabbings, head blows that led to concussions, and lungs irritated by bear and pepper spray. I was facing months of rehab, and I couldn't hug my wife or play ball with my son. Yet Republican leaders were going on TV to spin lies about the invasion. Didn't anyone take responsibility for their actions anymore?

"I can't stay quiet about what Trump's mob did to me and my team and all the spineless members of Congress still supporting him," I told Monica over the phone. "These motherfuckers were running scared for their lives while I risked mine protecting them on the front lines."

"You want to be a whistleblower?" she asked. She was afraid of the lunatic fringe. Who could blame her? Trump was famous for publicly attacking anyone who went against him. This was a guy who'd encouraged his mob of insurrectionists to hang his loyal vice president. What would he do to us?

"It's easy to figure out where we live," she said. "What if they find Manny's school?"

"I've been trying to teach you how to use a revolver. But you keep refusing," I told her.

"I'm not a police officer," she said. "I don't want to put my hand on a gun."

"But you should learn how, for protection."

"You can protect us by not calling attention to yourself," she argued.

"I'll try to respect your wishes," I said. "But I don't know how long I can keep quiet."

I texted Harry Dunn for the numbers of Brian Sicknick's mother, father, and fiancée, Sandra Garza, and phoned them the next day to offer my condolences.

It wasn't until Sunday night, when the COVID test came back negative, that I saw my son in person. I gave him a big kiss and hug. He held me close, not wanting to let go.

"I was so worried about you, Daddy," he said.

After eating our favorite toasted Panera Bread chicken sandwiches for dinner, we watched an old Gabriel Iglesias Netflix comedy special from my bed downstairs. I had my foot elevated and a pillow underneath my left arm. Manny leaned on my right shoulder so he wouldn't hurt me. Monica sat up on my other side. Iglesias riffed about how his fifteen-year-old son Frankie refused to wear deodorant until he mentioned it in a special and the kids at school spammed him with sticks of Ban, Irish Spring, and Dove.

"Think he's funny?" I asked Manny in Spanish, which we spoke at home to keep him bilingual.

"Hilarious," Manny said. "But don't ever embarrass me that way."

"Promise. I don't think his son likes it either."

After they went to sleep, I turned to the news, incensed by the propaganda the right-wing kept pushing.

FOR US, THE insurrection wasn't over.

On January 12, intel warned that all the bridges leading to Washington, D.C., were under threat of being blown up. Not long after, I heard two loud booms. Rushing to the Capitol's armory, heart racing, I issued rifles and rounds to my team as they responded to the fence the National Guard was manning. Officers were sent to investigate. Luckily, the explosion was caused by a homeless man using a propane tank to cook and heat up his tent, not insurrectionists.

The hits kept coming. Multiple alerts said rioters were returning for another round. Everything felt suspicious: a vehicle's muffler backfiring, someone with no ID. Conspiracy theories abounded. Someone from Trump's White House landline was accused of phoning a rioter around 4:30 p.m. on January 6, but nothing was proven. National Guard troops were in the same camouflage uniforms many rioters wore. We were ordered to double-check all identification, as the white nationalists might be impersonating soldiers to gain access.

One officer heard a soldier brag that he'd taken part in the riot and called his supervisor. The soldier's credentials were taken, and he was removed from Capitol Grounds. Altogether twelve National Guard troops were expelled from D.C. security details. Virginia Guard Jacob Fracker, an infantryman and ex-Marine, was the first former member of the U.S. military to be arrested for his role in the attack. He pleaded guilty and testified against his fellow Rocky Mount Police Department rioter Thomas Robertson. Their selfies and social media posts led to their arrests. After testifying against Robertson, the man he called "Dad," Fracker was sentenced to a year of probation, 59 days of home confinement and 120 hours of community service.

They were only two of many traitorous soldiers and police. During the riots I'd seen protesters wearing veterans hats and one in a sheriff's vest. I'd recognized the look of law enforcement by their clean-shaven short haircuts and toned physiques. Ironically, they'd worn BLUE LIVES MATTER T-shirts or blue ribbons signifying that they supported the force as they were beating us up. Poring over videos, I recognized a white guy in a green hat and THIN BLUE LINE wristband who I'd thought had been on the force helping us close the tunnel door. From the tape I now saw he'd been trying to trap us.

In all, more than 118 people with military backgrounds who rioted that day were eventually charged with crimes, most of them veterans, according to *The New York Times*. But three active duty marines who worked in intelligence—two sergeants and one corporal—faced charges of unlawfully entering the Capitol building and disorderly conduct. The cases are ongoing.

I kept reviewing my police reports to explain how I'd been assaulted by more than fifty assailants, with multiple simultaneous attacks. I studied footage sent by the FBI and the Capitol Police Investigation unit to identify myself and each assailant. Managers who saw me watching clips on my computer at work said, "Stop obsessing," "Let it go," and "Reliving that day isn't good for you." They didn't know I was participating in ongoing investigations. I was keeping my word to Monica. I wasn't yet ready to speak publicly, but I could assist with court trials and offer a written victim statement detailing every assault committed against me and my force.

Needing an overview for reports, witness statements, and testimony, I did research and calculated that more than 100,000 rioters on January 6 had quickly overwhelmed the 417 CDU Capitol Police on duty. Out of 1,879 of our officers, a high percentage weren't trained for riots or were sick with COVID, working remotely, or unaccounted for. Even after 850 Metropolitan Police reinforcements came, we were still vastly outnumbered. And it was unclear which officers on duty were turncoats. Michael Riley, a member of my own precinct, messaged a

rioter on Facebook about how not to get caught. Riley was later con-
victed of felony obstruction and resigned. I had to be careful at work. I
didn't know who I could trust.

It was disconcerting to learn that three days before the riot, internal
Capitol Police intel had revealed upcoming high security risks where
"Congress itself" could be the target. The memo, leaked to *The Washington Post*, said: "Supporters of the current president see January 6,
2021, as the last opportunity to overturn the results of the presidential
election. Stop the Steal's propensity to attract white supremacists, militia members and others who actively promote violence may lead to a
significantly dangerous situation for law enforcement and the general
public." The report notified top brass that organizers urged Trump supporters to come with guns, combat gear, gas masks, and military-style
bulletproof vests, noting that the protests were prompted by "President
Trump himself." An FBI office in Virginia had issued a warning that
extremists were preparing to travel to D.C., threatening to commit
violence and war.

In a stunning lack of communication and preparation, leadership
never transmitted that essential intel to me or my supervisors. Was
it denial, error, or something worse, like an internal conspiracy with
the rioters? The dangerously inadequate police reaction pointed to a
coverup of the racial component. That became obvious to me when a
Black lieutenant shared footage showing that most of us fighting in the
tunnel were officers of color.

"Do you notice there's not a lot of white police in there?" she asked.

"I fought alongside some white officers in the tunnel," I replied.
"In fact, Michael Fanone took my spot and almost died because of it."

On the other hand, nobody investigated the racial disparity to see
how many Caucasian officers helped the rioters or were simply pas-
sive and did nothing to keep them out. Most of our unions—like the
355,000-member-strong Fraternal Order of Police—endorsed Trump's
reelection. A high number of officers donated money to his campaign

through platforms like WinRed, to such an extent that Philadelphia Black law enforcement groups condemned the Trump support. I flashed to the show of might against BLM demonstrators six months before. If we'd had the same fierce response to Trump's white nationalists, nobody in blue would have died or been wounded.

Capitol Police Chief Steven Sund insisted he'd asked the House and Senate Sergeant at Arms for permission to declare an emergency and call in reinforcements six times during the attacks, but they'd rebuffed his requests. The National Guard didn't jump in until around 6:00 p.m., after the violence had ceased. Sund resigned after the siege, along with both sergeants-at-arms of the Senate and the House. I thought they were being scapegoated while Trump and the Republican representatives who'd abetted him escaped the blame they deserved. High-ranking members of Trump's own party finally publicly denounced him for causing a national security threat that almost shook down our government in the aftermath of the attack. To me, Trump was a monster they'd been feeding for four years, despite the cascade of warning signs.

"This was an intensifying crescendo of conspiracy theories orchestrated by an outgoing president who seemed determined to either overturn the voters' decision or else torch our institution on the way out," Senate Majority Leader Mitch McConnell said. "There is no question, none, that President Trump is practically and morally responsible for provoking the events of that day . . . A mob was assaulting the Capitol in his name . . . These criminals were carrying his banners, hanging his flags, and screaming their loyalty to him."

So I was appalled when the Senate voted 57–43 on February 13, 2021, to convict Trump on a charge of inciting insurrection, falling short of the two-thirds threshold needed to convict. Only seven Republican senators cast anti-Trump votes. After his speech, McConnell wimped out of voting against Trump for the lame reason that he believed it was unconstitutional to convict a president who was no longer in office. I was incensed by the duplicity of right-wing leaders like

Kevin McCarthy, who'd first vocally held Trump responsible for the insurrection, then flown down to Mar-a-Lago to make amends, back-pedaling the truth. Instead of dumping Trump, most of his constituents and leadership embraced him and kept kissing his ass.

It was unreal. As they minimized Trump's clear culpability, my belief in American values crumbled. It wasn't just politicians, but also my own colleagues. U.S. police unions never revoked their support for Trump or denounced him. This racist president—who'd bragged he could shoot someone on Fifth Avenue and not lose a vote—had just incited a modern civil war that almost killed me, and half the country was pretending it never happened.

What had I risked my life for?

23

Brave Enough

Washington, D.C., 2021

W E   W E R E   O N   H I G H   S E C U R I T Y   F O R   P R E S I D E N T Biden's inauguration on January 20. I escorted five National Guard snipers up a metal ladder and through a hatch on the roof of the Botanic Garden in case of attack. Then, on my police mountain bicycle, I patrolled the West Front, where just two weeks earlier we'd fought for our lives. Walking up the landing of the steps, I caught part of Biden's inspiring speech pleading for national unity. I'd been putting in double shifts and I was tired, but I also felt gratified that we'd accomplished our goal of allowing the peaceful transfer of power. I was moved by the twenty-two-year-old Black poet Amanda Gorman's powerful lines about the light we're brave enough to see—and be. Her verse provided a shocking contrast to the white nationalists who'd come to this place shouting, "It's time for war," "Stop the steal," and "Hang Mike Pence" while waving the Confederate flag, brandishing weapons, and trashing the seat of democracy.

Despite all the injuries we'd suffered, mental and physical, I was proud that we'd done our job of protecting the sacred electoral process, proving democracy won—though just barely.

That was the last time I wore my blue uniform for full duty.

After that I was out on restricted assignment, teleworking from my house and only going to the office periodically. Pandemic slowdowns meant it wasn't until March 5 that I could have my first surgery, bone fusion, to fix the two toes in my right foot with eight screws and a plate. Waiting until it healed before moving on to the next procedure, I focused on the administrative side of my job. The second operation repaired my rotator cuff and labrum tear as well as my bicep tendon. I followed the doctor's orders, but when I came home and stood up the next day, I heard two pops in my left shoulder. My tendon contracted so badly that my bulging bicep looked disfigured. It was a Friday. I immediately called the doctor, but he couldn't see me until Monday.

"Stop overextending yourself!" Monica scolded me.

"I didn't!" I argued. "I just tried to stand using my right arm, the way the doctor instructed."

"Your arm has been weakened," Dr. Hampton told me the following week. "The surgery was very delicate."

"When can I get it fixed?"

"I can't guarantee I can fix it," he told me. "It's not a big deal. After Bronco John Elway had the same surgery, his bicep tendon contracted but he still played football and won a championship."

"Yeah, but I'm not a quarterback," I told him. "And my arm looks like Popeye's."

"Well, you just might have to give up your modeling career," he said, sarcastically.

His flippancy was annoying, but I took it to mean I'd eventually regain my strength and be able to resume all my job responsibilities. I wished everything would go back to normal faster. So far, the grueling two-hour physical therapy twice a week—with ice and swimming—wasn't healing the chronic pain in my shoulder and foot. Nor did it increase the motion in my left arm. I could only sleep three or four hours a night, and even that required uncomfortably elevating my foot and sandwiching pillows between my arms and torso to avoid reinjury. My recovery was slower than we expected. Since I couldn't exercise every day as usual, I gained twenty-five pounds over six months.

Monica had to help me dress and eat and drive me to the doctor and physical therapy. After missing a second semester of medical school, she put her career on hold to take care of me. I couldn't coach my son in basketball, so he stopped playing, refusing to set foot on the court without me. Hugging Manny or my wife, I winced in agony. My mood spiraled. Unable to work nights and overtime, my salary diminished; I canceled the family vacation we'd planned to see my grandparents in the Caribbean.

I was humbled when Democratic Representative Jamie Raskin, comedian Jon Stewart, and President Biden publicly called out the bravery of the police officers who'd been brutalized during the insurrection. Yet their commendations didn't compensate for my losses. I hated feeling deformed and demoted. I'd lost a quarter of my pay as a result of the heroism I was being praised for.

Lieutenant Reid called every week to check on me. He was the rare exception. In general, there was a shocking lack of guidance or empathy from the force. I'd been the victim of vicious assaults on the job that were captured in pictures and videotape. I had witnessed countless crimes the police and Congress asked me to attest to, which took hundreds of hours. After working with the FBI, I had a perfunctory phone call with a coordinator from their Victim Services program. Yet nobody offered financial aid or professional advice to assist me and my family during this medical, career, and spiritual catastrophe. It stung. When four of my officers quit the department, I was the one who shared info on how they could get assistance from the Public

Safety Officers' Benefits and D.C. Crime Victims Compensation programs, and offered good job references. Several confessed they were having a tough time dealing with physical and psychological trauma as well as less income.

I preferred seeing myself as a strong leader, not a bitter, victimized ball of rage, but I couldn't deny that I was in a dark place. I was defeated and isolated, stunned that few seemed willing to admit just how close the attackers came to destroying us. I couldn't eat or sleep well, I was moving more slowly, and my whole body ached from wounds that weren't healing.

On February 22, 2021, home with my foot in a medical boot, elevated on pillows, and wrapped in a motorized ice therapy machine for swelling, I turned on the TV to catch my old buddy Harry Dunn giving an interview to ABC News correspondent Pierre Thomas. In a sports cap, with gray in his beard, Harry looked terrified. Asked to describe what he'd observed at the Capitol on January 6, he said:

> You just see a sea of people, Trump flags, Confederate flags, blue line flags, you see officers fighting with these people, pepper sprayed, smoke grenades, gas grenades, pepper balls . . . We fought these people who were prepared . . . they had on gas masks, body armor, two-way radios, bulletproof vests, they were ready to go . . . I was absolutely scared . . . I'm a big guy, I'm six foot seven, this giant person. And we had our guns out and I'm thinking all these people, they're armed too . . . They're going to take me out . . . A large number of people in this crowd were racists . . . It wasn't just a mob or a bunch of thugs, they were terrorists. Their goal was to disrupt this country's democracy. I was called a "nigger" a couple dozen times . . . protecting this building. Is this America?

When I returned to do office work for a week, I overheard a conversation between fellow sergeants: "Dunn made it seem like it was all about race," one complained when he knew I was on the other side of the cubicle.

"All that happened to Harry Dunn was he got called a racial slur. He's taking advantage of it," another sergeant said.

"Maybe you don't know what happened since you weren't even here that day," I shot back.

These were the guys—the same white guys—who'd laughed at and quoted Trump's xenophobic slanders about "the China Virus" and "Kung Flu"—derogatory terms for COVID—while supervising our diverse division.

I'd experienced the same fighting, fear, and racism as Harry, so I felt grateful for his candor. "Good for you for coming forward," I'd texted Dunn. "Proud to know you, bro. It was powerful when you looked right into the camera and said 'You tried to overthrow our democracy. You failed.'"

"Thank you, buddy. How are you doing?" he asked.

"I'm okay," I lied.

Harry's testimony was impactful and important, but the TV commentator made it clear that he was speaking just for himself and not for the department. Our leadership should have denounced the crimes committed against our police force, yet Harry—a private first class—was the only one out there on a limb at this point, exposing an important side of the story. I feared a majority of Americans might not believe the horrors we'd survived because he'd focused on his own experience of racial derision and not the invasion's goal of stopping the transfer of presidential power.

Because I was higher ranked than Harry, an army veteran, and someone who'd sustained serious physical injuries—with scars, X-rays, and videos for proof—I imagined more people would pay attention if I told my story too. If I joined Harry, he wouldn't be standing on an island alone, and it would encourage other officers to also come forward. Monica was understandably hesitant.

"What if you lose your job?" she asked.

"Then I'll do something else. I'll start a restaurant like my mom. I've done it before."

"What if they bully Manny at school?"

"I won't let them," I assured her.

Heeding her wishes, I kept quiet, sweating through physical therapy, working part-time. But staying bottled up took a toll and made me more tense and easily aggravated. After my son put out his hand to help me into the car, I snapped at him. Then I felt horrible and called the doctor who'd treated my PTSD from the army. Overbooked from the pandemic, she recommended a psychiatrist I saw virtually twice a week.

"Staying silent is wrecking me inside," I confessed to Dr. Polizzi. "I can't even do sports or play basketball to release the tension, like I used to. I'm so infuriated by the lies and deception, I feel like I could explode."

"Speaking out may really help you heal. But discuss your wife's concerns with her first," she advised.

"I've tried to keep quiet, but I can't anymore," I told Monica, as we spoke in our usual Spanish over dinner one night.

"You already know exactly how I feel about this, sir," she said in perfect English; that was how I knew she was pissed off at me.

ONE SATURDAY NIGHT in February, I was taken off guard when my mother, father, Uncle Federico, Aunt Victoria, and brothers Tony and Giovanny showed up at my house without calling, in a three-car caravan from Brooklyn and Pennsylvania, carrying Dominican rice, beans, and chicken. They walked in wearing light blue COVID masks, though everyone was vaccinated. Monica, Manny, and I put on masks too. Milo was barking like crazy, excited to jump on and slobber over these relatives he'd never met.

Mom tried to hug me, but I winced and said, "Be careful of my shoulder."

"We saw what happened on TV and we want to support you," Dad said.

"We want to make sure you're okay," Tony told me. "We can pay some bills or mow the lawn. Whatever you need."

"We're here to help," Dad said, putting a few hundred-dollar bills in his hand when we shook.

"No, I'm good, thanks. Send it to Grandma Andrea," I told them.

"Your house is so big and beautiful," Aunt Victoria said. "Can we get a tour?"

Limping with the black boot on my foot, I took them around. Dad and Federico were impressed with the grill on the patio in our back-yard. I pointed to the vegetables I'd been growing.

"You should grow corn," Dad suggested.

"And eggplant too," Mom added.

I was glad my parents had stayed friends while they'd both found other partners that made them happier. I'd visited Dad in New York and we spoke on the phone every few weeks. But the last time he'd been in Virginia was for my wedding in 2010. It was the first time Uncle Federico and his sister Victoria were meeting Manny. I felt guilty and regretted waiting so long, for an emergency, to see everyone. I was touched that the relatives I'd run away from were now my supporting cast, bringing me food and offering me money and to cut my grass.

As my aunt, Mom, and Monica heated up the food, the men sat around on the beige living room couches having a few beers. Although I'd avoided alcohol because of the medication I was on, they convinced me to have one Presidente.

"Where were you hurt?" Dad asked, and I showed him my foot and arm.

"I can't believe all those people believed Trump's lies. Look what they did to you." Uncle Federico shook his head in disgust.

"I can't believe it either," I agreed. "Trump lies with every breath he takes. Everyone needs to stop defending him."

"But there were irregularities in the voting," Giovanny commented.

I turned and looked at him, the hairs on my back standing up. "Even if that were true—and it's not—it wouldn't give anyone the right to take matters into their own hands and beat up police officers in full uniform!" I raised my voice. "Here I am, still battered. I can barely walk or dress myself. I'm lucky to be alive."

"There's a lot of news reports saying the protests were started by Black Lives Matter and Antifa," he argued defensively, repeating inane right-wing conspiracy theories he'd probably heard on Fox News. Even members of my own Latino brood were still making excuses for the rich, elitist, criminally negligent ex-president. It was maddening.

"Look, that's bullshit. I was there, on the front lines!" I shouted, remembering why I'd needed to escape my *familia*. "I did not see one Black Lives Matter or Antifa protester there. They were all Trump supporters, armed, in MAGA hats. And I didn't watch it on TV or read about it on the internet. I nearly died multiple times and I have the injuries to prove it!"

"Time to change the subject," Dad interrupted, chilling us out. "Let's not talk politics."

Instead, they asked how they could help me and whether I was getting compensated, trying to figure out how to pull it together to assist financially.

"Workers' comp is still paying me most of my salary. Don't worry. We'll be fine." I wasn't sure who I was trying to convince. Maybe myself.

They all stayed overnight, sleeping in our extra bedroom and on the living room's pullout sofa, couches, and an inflatable air mattress. Sunday afternoon we posed for pictures before they left.

Underneath the American flag by the front door, Mom cried as she gave me a big hug. "I wish I lived closer so I could help take care of you," she whispered.

"That was sweet they all came down to see you," Monica said later.

"I hope they all come back again soon," I admitted.

I wished some things would have been different growing up. But in their own way I knew my relatives really loved me and made me who I was. I was touched to remember how, despite everything, my family always helped each other out in a crisis.

Although the rest of the world appeared eager to move on, for officers who'd been traumatized by the insurrection, the crisis was ongoing and never ending. Learning that policemen Jeffrey Smith, Howard S. Liebengood, Kyle DeFreytag, and later Gunther Hashida died by suicide after fighting off the Capitol attackers, I felt haunted. Howard's wife wrote to her representative complaining that her husband had been called back to work "practically around the clock" on January 7, causing severe sleep deprivation. Smith's widow Erin said that despite complaining he wasn't feeling well, Jeffrey's doctor had released him too soon. He pulled his car over on the way to work one morning and squeezed the trigger.

I knew firsthand the dangers of repression and depression. In Iraq, when suffering from exhaustion, frustration, and PTSD, I'd almost turned my weapon on myself. I never told Monica how bad it got in Iraq, but after reading about the suicidal wave, she watched me carefully, unnerved.

TWICE A YEAR, everyone on the force had to take a test at the range for weapon certification. We had to score at least 208 out of 300 to keep our guns. I'd been due to take the test on January 8, 2021. Because of the insurrection and my injuries, I'd missed the deadline and still couldn't shoot. The range sergeant, an old friend from my rookie years, called me from the basement.

"You weren't certified last cycle, you missed the qualification date," she said.

I wasn't surprised. I might have even felt relief. In March 2021, days before my first surgery, I went to the Rayburn Building's basement gun range. Removing my handgun from my off-duty holster, I gave it to the range sergeant.

"I'm turning in my Glock 22," I said, hoping I could get it back when I fully recovered.

After disappointing medical results, I didn't think I was ready to pass the upcoming weapon qualification test. In the army I'd fired my gun in a sting, though as far as I knew I'd never hit or killed anyone. On the force, I'd only drawn my gun once, when I was threatened by a suspect in a dark overpass, but my backup helped me apprehend the suspect without shooting. Giving up my firearm—even temporarily— made me feel vulnerable and unprotected.

"Let me get some paperwork for you to fill out," the sergeant said. "I need your badge and all four magazines with all the bullets."

Returning my badge and bullets the next day was a stark reminder of how much my wounds had ruined my work. I signed the property receipt. She gave me a copy. It seemed unfair, not the way I'd ever expected work to go. Yet, walking up the stairs and heading back outside, I felt lighter and a little liberated not having to carry around my gun for a while, with no chance to use it on myself, or anyone else.

"I turned in my weapon today," I told Monica.

"Why?"

"They required me to," I explained, "since my injuries mean I can't pass the weapons test."

"If you go public, what if Trump supporters show up at our house to harass us?" she asked.

"Then we'll call the police."

To make her feel safer, I erected a higher fence around our house and installed security cameras and motion sensor lights. Then I went to a local gun store. The paperwork and background check only took fifteen minutes, and I walked out with a new Glock in its black case. At home, I stored it in the same safe where I'd kept my department-issued weapon and told Monica where it was, in case she needed it when I wasn't around.

"Just make sure you lock the safe," she said. I did.

My lawyer recommended a company that erased my online presence. My home and work address, personal history, and public records were expunged. Still, I was anxious. For the first time in sixteen years, I wasn't officially an armed police officer. On family and medical leave, I was receiving 75 percent of my salary and would still be a member of the police force, but I couldn't wear my uniform, respond to emergency calls, or make arrests. I walked around in plain clothes with just my radio and official ID, feeling like I'd regressed back to my old security guard job in New York. I continued to testify for the district attorney and federal courts prosecuting the rioters, in limbo until I could go back to policing full-time.

In June 2021, glued to the news, I was sickened to hear Republican leaders Lindsey Graham, Jim Jordan, Marjorie Taylor Greene, Josh Hawley, and Donald Trump peddling the ongoing deception that the insurrection was a peaceful protest. They claimed they led the party of law and order, supporting police and veterans, publicly thanking us for our service. But behind closed doors, they were power-hungry liars who betrayed their protectors for political gain. It galled me every time they called the deranged criminals who'd assaulted me in uniform "patriots."

Even when I'd disagreed with their political stances, I used to think all leaders from the United States were honorable and would do what was right for the country, the way John McCain had broken from his own party lines, earning him the title "maverick." I'd once naively believed that a true patriot obeyed the chain of command and rules to the letter. But now I realized that exposing government injustice was more essential. I felt I had the obligation to follow justice and not any false authority desecrating it. As an immigrant, I took seriously my pledge to defend and protect the Constitution of the United States against foreign and domestic threats. Even if that threat was the president, the police, and the members of Congress who abetted him.

At noon on June 3, I caught Harry Dunn speaking out again on CNN. I texted him. "Give me a call whenever you can."

"I'm at lunch with friends," he responded right away. "I'll call in a few minutes."

"I can't believe nobody else is backing you up," I told him. "I'm ready to come forward too."

"I just did an interview with CNN reporter Whitney Wild, she's great," he said over the phone. "She's their law enforcement correspondent."

"Get her here within an hour. I'm ready to talk."

By 2:30 p.m. Wild was at my house. Nothing would ever be the same.

24

"Why Did the President Lie?"

Washington, D.C., June 2021

O<small>N</small> F<small>RIDAY</small> <small>NIGHT</small>, J<small>UNE</small> 4, M<small>ONICA</small>, M<small>ANNY</small>, <small>AND</small> I sat on the same bed where we'd watched Gabriel Iglesias. Only this time it wasn't funny. Instead of viewing another Netflix comedy special, we were watching me cry on national television.

"They called us traitors. They beat us. They dragged us," I told CNN reporter Whitney Wild in my first television interview. "I was very scared. I thought I was going to lose my life right there. I could hear my fellow officers screaming in agony. All I thought was I couldn't let them get in or there'd be a slaughter inside . . . I could hear the rioters scream 'We're going to shoot you. We're going to kill you. You're choosing your paycheck over the country. You're a disgrace. You're a traitor.'"

In high school, Ms. Vega had once asked if I'd speak in front of the school assembly. I'd told her, "No, it would be way too much pressure."

Self-conscious about my accent and indoctrinated to stay out of the limelight and not court trouble, I certainly never wanted to call attention to myself. But now, despite how traumatizing it was to relive the four hours of battle that brutalized me, it felt like a necessity, with no way around exposing the truth. The reason many people didn't do the right thing was because it hurt. But you couldn't be honest only when it was comfortable and convenient. I saw this interview as an extension of my service to my country. After all, I'd said in my Oath of Enlistment, "I do solemnly swear that I will support and defend the Constitution of the United States against all enemies, foreign and domestic; that I will bear true faith and allegiance to the same."

I worried the network would cut my footage badly or demean or mispresent me, but they didn't. I thought I came across as raw, unpolished, and still very emotional over the whole ordeal, but real.

"Hopefully everyone will now know what happened and can't keep denying it. I'm proud you did this," Monica said, holding me close, coming around despite being completely out of her comfort zone.

"You did good, Daddy," Manny told me, reaching over to hug me too.

Right beforehand, I'd left messages for the police's Public Information Officer and for Lieutenant Reid, giving them both a heads-up that I was doing the interview. I didn't want them caught unaware in case the higher-ups complained.

"Thanks for letting me know," Reid said.

Twenty-four hours after my segment aired, my deputy chief called. "The acting chief of police wanted me to reach out to you," he told me.

That sounded to me like he'd been ordered to make sure I wasn't suicidal, more concerned with the optics for the department than my health and well-being.

"I'm okay, though stressed out and battered," I told him. "But I didn't disparage the department, if that's what you guys are worried about."

"We wanted to make sure you're okay, since your message sounded distressed and frustrated."

"It was," I admitted.

"Stop watching the news all the time," he advised me.

"How can I not? I want to be back on the job full-time already. It's hard seeing everything from afar since the inauguration." Even doing the after-action review over the phone with a CDU commander, I felt like I needed to be there to explain better and improve our response in the future.

"Let us know how we can help," he said, rushing off the phone.

It felt like too little, too late. Especially when I returned to the office to do paperwork that week and said my usual "Hey, how are you?" to colleagues. Several supervisors kept walking, like I wasn't there, giving me the silent treatment. I didn't know if it was because I was one of the few to go public, or some of the rank and file disagreed with something I said, or both. It seemed like they were retaliating against me for speaking out.

"Your interview was awesome. Good for you. I'm glad you told your story," Harry told me, offering the unadulterated support I needed.

We expected more officers, police leaders, and politicians to come forward. That didn't happen. When I bumped into Ted Cruz, Josh Hawley, and Lindsey Graham in the hallways and elevators at the Capitol, they cravenly pretended not to see me, not acknowledging that I'd put my life on the line to protect theirs. After we'd cleared the Capitol of rioters on January 6, Cruz and Hawley still challenged the election results. Graham—who once tweeted "If we nominate Trump, we will get destroyed . . . and we will deserve it"—helped find a lawyer for Trump's second impeachment trial, blamed Nancy Pelosi for the pro-Trump violence, and whined about the Democrats' "brazen politicization of January 6," as if a political coup to overturn our election could be anything but politicized.

A white coworker insisted that left-wing protesters were involved in the Capitol melee, swearing she saw a rioter at the Rotunda in an Antifa shirt underneath a decoy Trump 2020 shirt—continuing the bald-faced deception.

"Where I was, for four hours, I did not see one BLM or Antifa protester," I told her. "Not one. Had they been there, they would have been lynched by the white nationalists."

After I cried giving testimony about January 6 that was televised, Fox News hosts Laura Ingraham and Tucker Carlson sarcastically mocked me and Harry Dunn on air, cutting out the clips where Harry revealed the racial abuse he suffered at the insurrection. Worse, Ingraham glorified white seventeen-year-old Kyle Rittenhouse for killing two unarmed protesters in Kenosha, Wisconsin. A wannabe vigilante with an AR-15 style rifle who killed two people and then sobbed in court to get leniency was Fox's hero, not the officers who'd held the police line and hadn't opened fire—though, unlike Rittenhouse, we had provocation and full authority to intervene. Two right-wing representatives even offered Rittenhouse congressional internships, which meant that one day I might have to protect him too. And I would, because it was my sworn duty.

I thought of the shooting of Congressman Steve Scalise in Alexandria in 2017, when a lone gunman distraught over President Trump's election opened fire on members of the Republican congressional baseball team. Trump condemned the "very, very brutal assault," and leaders honored the five Capitol officers who took down Scalise's attackers—one who was wounded. Nancy Pelosi called the officers' actions "an inspiration to us all."

Yet now, twenty-one members of the GOP voted no on the bill to award the Congressional Gold Medal to January 6 officers who'd risked their lives, even though it still passed. Representative Adam Kinzinger publicly criticized his colleagues, tweeting, "How you can vote no to this is beyond me. Then again, denying an insurrection is as well. To the brave Capitol (and DC metro PD) thank you. To the 21: they will continue to defend your right to vote no anyway."

The partisan reactions to January 6 continued to be divisive. At my office, a colleague repeated Ingraham's slurs about my accent and tears, saying, "Like Dunn, he's just seeking the spotlight."

"How many hours did you spend fighting the mob in the tunnel? Sergeant Gonell spent four hours and nearly died. He has done more for our country than most people who were born here!" Lieutenant Reid defended me.

Later, he took me aside and explained his theory to me. "Some officers here are still processing it and deal with it differently. Hearing you talk about it on TV makes it harder for them to move on. But it's fair and understandable that you want to hold the rioters accountable for what they did to you."

Many letters and emails came in from citizens across the world who supported me and wished me a speedy recovery. More interview requests followed. I accepted. To make sure I wouldn't get into legal trouble speaking out, I met with Harry's lawyer, who offered to handle me pro bono.

Over the summer, Monica told me that Manny asked her, "Why is Dad going on TV again? It's painful to watch."

"Because he wants those responsible to be held accountable," she'd told him.

Trying to shield my son, I realized I hadn't explained well enough why I was going public. I asked him to come with me to walk Milo after school the next day.

"You asked me why those people invaded the Capitol," I told him. "They wanted to win the election at all costs, despite not having the votes. The former president and his friends led the public to believe a lot of lies, despite the evidence. So thousands of rioters went to the Capitol to fight, believing what the president told them. I was injured doing my job to protect the politicians who were inside. Do you understand?"

"Why did the president lie?" he asked.

"You know how when you play basketball, you don't like to lose? And I tell you never be a sore loser. You can't win all the time. When you don't, you just try harder next time. Well, some adults need to learn that lesson too," I told him. "When you get older, you'll read more about the story in a history book one day."

"When I read it, I'll tell them, 'That was my dad,'" he said.

25

The Verdict

Washington, D.C., July 2021

WHEN I FIRST CAME TO THIS COUNTRY AS A KID, I had to go to school, learn a new language, and hustle to earn money for my family. That pattern continued in the army. On the force, I routinely worked sixteen-hour days. For the first time, I was taking a break. It gave me room to reconsider my career, how to build on my past success and achieve more security for my family. I'd always viewed my deep accent and mispronunciations of English as a disadvantage, keeping me from promotions on the force. During my recovery, in between therapies, I questioned that assumption. Perhaps the only thing holding me back was myself. I decided to take the lieutenant's test. I'd always secretly coveted joining the ranks of police brass. I knew making a full recovery and getting promoted was ambitious, but having a specific goal kept me motivated. I did well on the written part of the exam and even better on the scenario-based section, earning a top score that meant I had a good chance of getting chosen. Despite my injuries, I felt capable of fulfilling the higher role since it would be more of a desk job with mainly administrative duties.

"I'm going to take your spot when you get transferred," I teased Lieutenant Reid on a phone call after learning I'd passed.

"I look forward to working with you," he told me.

"All the headaches you put me through were worth it," I said. "But I'll need a lot of help."

Unfortunately, my joy evaporated later that day when my surgeon, Dr. Hampton, told me that there wasn't anything else he could do for me.

"But I still have problems with my left shoulder," I told him. "I need to be able to shoot a gun for my job or handcuff a suspect resisting arrest."

"You have a 68 percent range of motion, most people have 90 percent. You just have to learn to live with your disabilities now," he said. "I don't recommend you stay on the force. There are other things you can do beside policing."

Easy for him to say. What if his hand was maimed and someone commented, "Hey, just get another job, bro. No biggie." In sixteen years, I'd never once considered a different career. The thought was terrifying.

"I'm releasing you from physical therapy," my physical therapist Sheryl Johnson told me. "You're just not making any more progress."

"Get away from the Capitol," my psychiatrist Jennie Polizzi recommended. "Work somewhere else."

"Why?" I was flabbergasted. "I thought all this therapy was helping me get better."

"It is, but at the Capitol, you keep getting triggered. You were unnerved when someone taped a picture of Trump behind your computer, as if they were mocking you," she reminded me. "And at Costco when you bumped into a midnight shift coworker who asked you, 'When are you going to stop crying on TV?' you had to refrain from punching him."

"How about a desk job with the House or Senate sergeant-at-arms, using my military and police expertise?" I asked.

She shook her head. "Stay away from the Capitol for a year or two—until you heal. Down the road you can come back as a civilian. But there's a reason everyone is telling you to leave."

It was hard to hear the trio of professionals on my side all insist that my injuries meant I would never again be able to perform the duties of the job I loved. I was shattered. The timing was mind-blowing. At forty-two, I was only seven years shy of retirement. Right after the thrill of passing the lieutenant's test that would lead me to the highest rank and salary of my life, the bad news felt like three final nails in my coffin. While several officers I'd worked with just resigned to cut their losses and start over somewhere else, I couldn't even leave the job to mourn my defeat in private. I had to wait in purgatory until my retirement with disability was approved so I could take care of my family.

But at least someone still wanted me. In July 2021, I received a call and letter from the January 6th Committee, saying they'd seen me on CNN and requesting a meeting as soon as possible.

"They want me to testify before Congress. This record will be part of history," I told Monica. "I need to publicly identify as many of the assailants who assaulted me as I can, so they can hold the attackers accountable."

"Are you sure?" She was worried. "I know it's important they invited you. But only do it if you feel comfortable."

"Yes, of course I'll do it," I told my lawyer.

I wore civilian clothes to the three-hour briefing, which my lawyer attended with me. Although I'd already turned in my weapon and was technically on restricted duty, I asked the deputy chief if I could wear my uniform for the official testimony.

"I don't think it's possible," he said.

"Let Nancy Pelosi know," I instructed my lawyer, assuming

televised testimony would be more powerful coming from a policeman in his work blues and badge.

The chief relented, phoning to say, "Okay, you're allowed to wear your uniform. Get your badge and wallet back from the Property Office. But only for the testimony. Return it the next day."

"What about my gun?" I asked, wanting to be fully reinstated to who I was and should still be.

"Office of General Counsel said no," he responded before transferring the call to a different department.

At 7:00 A.M. on July 28, a few days after my forty-second birthday, I went to my bedroom closet, where my dress uniform—along with three more—hung. Monica had complained it was so crowded with my police gear, she had to keep all of her clothes in the guest room closet. I put on my Class A dark blue pants. She had to help me get the long-sleeve shirt over my arm since my shoulder was still sore, along with clipping on the blue tie. My injured foot was still too swollen for my regular police boots. I tried on four different pairs that were all uncomfortable and wound up wearing my black basketball shoes, leaving the right sneaker looser than the left. She'd already decided not to accompany me to the Cannon Building in the Capitol Complex, but I asked again.

"No, I don't want to be publicly identified on television," she repeated.

"I'll drive myself then," I said.

"Are you sure that's safe?"

"My doctor released me to drive," I reminded her. "I'll go slow."

Driving forty-five miles an hour on I-95, I still arrived an hour early. Cameras, photographers, and reporters were everywhere; it was a frenzy. The hearing was scheduled to last four hours and was broadcast live. Harry Dunn, Michael Fanone, Daniel Hodges, and I were each given five minutes to share a statement. I tried to speak slowly and clearly so people would understand my words. I wasn't nervous, but I wrote down what I planned to say, so I wouldn't forget anything important, yet even as I read my prepared remarks, I kept adding more things. There was so much I wanted to explain. I went over the time limit, but nobody stopped me.

During the questioning, when they showed me videos of the attacks, I identified myself in almost every frame. I tried to keep my composure but welled up when they showed my bloody hands in the riot where I'd almost died.

Later, I would applaud Representative Liz Cheney when she said in June 2022, "Tonight I say this to my Republican colleagues who are defending the indefensible: there will come a day when Donald Trump is gone, but your dishonor will remain."

Now, after all nine members of the Committee approached us, we shook hands.

"Thank you for defending the Capitol and protecting us," Cheney told me.

Adam Kinzinger, who'd been a lieutenant colonel in the Air National Guard, said, "I wish I'd done my overseas tour of duty with you. I know you'd have my back."

While my views sometimes clashed with Cheney's and Kinzinger's, I admired that they put the safety of our democracy over their ideologies. Of the 265 elected Republicans in Congress, they were the only two who ever thanked me.

Finishing my testimony, I revealed the final recommendations from my doctors. In July 2022, at the end of another Committee hearing, Congressman Jamie Raskin brought it up on national television:

> A violent insurrection to overturn an election is not an
> abstract thing . . . hundreds of people were bloodied,

injured, and wounded in the process, including more than 150 police officers—some of them sitting in this room today. I want to give you an update on one officer who was badly wounded in the attack and is well known to members of this Committee because he testified before us last year. Sergeant Aquilino Gonell is an army veteran who spent a year on active combat duty in the Iraq War and then 16 years on the Capitol force. Nothing he ever saw in combat in Iraq . . . prepared him for the insurrection where he was savagely beaten, punched, pushed, kicked, shoved, stomped, and sprayed with chemical irritants, along with other officers, by members of a mob carrying hammers, knives, batons, and police shields taken by force and wielding the American flag against police officers as a dangerous weapon . . . Sergeant Gonell's team of doctors told him that permanent injuries he has suffered on his left shoulder and right foot now make it impossible for him to continue as a police officer. He must leave policing for good and figure out the rest of his life. Sergeant Gonell, we wish you and your family all the best, we are here for you, and we salute you for your valor, your eloquence, and your beautiful commitment to America. I wonder what former President Trump would say to someone like Sergeant Gonell, who must now go about remaking his life. I wonder if he could even understand what motivates a patriot like Sergeant Gonell.

Hearing Representative Raskin publicly announce that I'd have to leave the force made it seem intensely final. I felt like something was taken away from me, like part of me was dying. I rushed outside the double guarded doors, sweating and dizzy, having trouble breathing, feeling on the verge of a panic attack. Harry followed me out. With his giant octopus arms wrapped around me he said, "I got you. You're going to be good, Sarge. Everything is going to work out."

How confusing it was to hear government leaders praise me for "valiantly" fulfilling my duty while my injuries were keeping me from doing my job. I appreciated the recognition of my courage, yet gratitude wasn't paying the bills. I went to each public Committee hearing with officers Harry and Michael and Brian Sicknick's family and his fiancée, Sandra Garza, in solidarity. The only session I missed was the day of Manny's basketball game at school. I'd already told him I would go. No way would I break that promise.

After one of the hearings, Sandra asked me, "How are you holding up?"

"Not so great," I confessed. "I haven't recovered from my surgeries. I'm still stressed out from everything that happened. Now I have to worry how I'll earn a living if I can't work on the force anymore. And it's screwed up my wife's career too."

Days later, an envelope came in the mail from Sandra. It turned out that she'd received a charity grant through the Capitol Police Memorial Fund that she generously shared with other officers in need. She'd sent me a check to help get me through my medical ordeals.

"I can't take this. I didn't open up about my problems because I wanted anything from you," I told her over the phone, ashamed that our family bank account had dwindled to $1,300 while bills kept coming.

She insisted. Broke and broken, I swallowed my pride and accepted. It felt like Brian was lending me a hand from beyond.

26

Strong Constitution

Washington, D.C., July 2021

GATHERED MY HANDCUFFS, UTILITY BELT, BLACK BOOTS, and four different uniforms, all the police equipment I'd been issued over the years. It felt like a divorce I didn't want.

"Put it all in a bag and tell them to come get it," advised Michael Fanone. "If they don't, put it in the trash. Tell them thanks but fuck you for not protecting us."

With so much D.C. doublespeak, Michael's honesty and unadulterated anger was refreshing to hear. But I wanted to end my sixteen-year tour of duty the way I'd started it: following regulations and going by the book, showing respect for the force. So I carried two suitcases with my police clothes to the USCP Property Division at the Government Printing Office. Letting go of the gear that meant so much to me was disorienting. It seemed like I was being punished, forced to return my identity. Who would I be without it? The building was a mile from where I worked, so I was glad I didn't have to see my colleagues or say

goodbye yet. I would save that for the formal last day, when I'd officially receive my walking papers.

BEFORE I LEFT for good, I did break protocol once. That was when I
saw chairman of the Joint Chiefs of Staff Mark A. Milley, the Defense
Department's top uniformed officer, on the second floor of the Capitol
near the Rayburn Room, across the hallway from the House Chamber. I was on my way to the Rotunda to attend an event for Hershel
W. "Woody" Williams, the last remaining Medal of Honor recipient
from World War II, when I spotted Milley.

The sixty-four-year-old general, who'd led troops in Afghanistan
and Iraq, became one of my heroes when he gave sworn testimony to
the January 6th Committee that rhetorically called out Trump: "You
know, Commander in Chief, you got an assault going on on the Capitol of the United States of America. And there's nothing? No call?
Nothing? Zero?" He revealed that Vice President Mike Pence—not
Trump—made efforts to secure the Capitol so it could resume its joint
session, phoning military leaders and the National Guard. Milley had
blatantly accused Trump of "doing great and irreparable harm" to the
country by politicizing the military, insisting the ex-president and his
men "shook the very republic to its core. Can you imagine what a
group of people who are much more capable could have done?" he'd
asked.

I was not supposed to stop the general as he was en route to a meeting, with my captain escorting him. Doing so wasn't professional. Yet,
starstruck, I thought, *Fuck it, I'm leaving the job anyway.* I followed him
into an elevator. When he stepped out at the basement of the Capitol,
I called to him, "Hey, General, I just wanted to say thank you for your
military service and January 6th testimony."

"I recognize you. I know who you are," he responded. "I appreciate
what you did too."

He gave me his business card. "Whatever you need, you give me a call. I can't make miracles, but I do know a few people," he told me.

He then turned and asked his assistant to give him a challenge coin with 20TH CHAIRMAN JOINT CHIEFS OF STAFF and his name on it. Giving one out was a way to show appreciation for a job well done. As we shook hands, he put the coin in his palm, transferring it into mine. I was touched by the gesture.

"You see this?" He pointed to the tiny Constitution etched on the coin with the words WE THE PEOPLE OF THE UNITED STATES. He told me, "We follow this and we keep our oath to it. Not to any one person but to the Constitution. You kept your oath, both home and abroad. Thank you for defending it."

"It's an honor to meet you," I went on. I couldn't help but add, "And I really admire that you spoke out against Trump."

"The honor is mine, Soldier and Staff Sergeant Gonell. And everyone will be held accountable one way or the other. Trust me," he said before walking ahead.

"What the hell are you doing, dude?" my police captain hissed through gritted teeth, his face turning red.

"Look, before I leave the force, I wanted to meet him," I told him.

He rolled his eyes, flabbergasted by my fanboy move. But the indestructible façade I'd cultivated in the military and police force was melting. I wasn't afraid to be vulnerable, or human.

I felt a little less forlorn about leaving the job when the assistant chief of police phoned to tell me, "There's a trip to the White House coming up for the Gold Medal signing. You've been chosen to go." I was pleased to be one of the twenty officers asked to attend the event with Harry, Michael, Daniel Hodges, Thomas Rhodes, and Caroline Edwards. Sandra would also be honored, as well as families of the men we'd lost to suicide. Monica and Manny could come as my guests.

At the White House on August 5, 2021, I was startled that

President Biden repeated the phrase I'd used during my interview with the January 6th Committee, describing the insurrection as "a medieval battle."

Shaking hands with Biden, I reminded him of the previous times we'd met when he was a senator and vice president. "I've taken pictures at the Capitol with you before."

"Thank you for your service, here and abroad," he said. "I was very moved by your testimony. You said it best—it was a horrific medieval battle."

What a thrill to hear the U.S. president again quote my words. More thrilling was having my son see me celebrated at the Rose Garden. Sitting next to me, Manny wore khakis and a blue vest and tie like mine. During the ceremony, he stared up at me, starry-eyed, tapping my shoulder and whispering, "I'm proud of you" in English, then a bit later he said it in Spanish too. *"Estoy orgulloso de ti, papi."*

"Thanks, Manny."

"But my friends aren't going to believe we're at the White House," he added. "So we need to take some pictures."

We posed—fully masked—with the president, Vice President Harris, and Nancy Pelosi, who was the first one—aside from me—to mention my wife's sacrifices. I felt privileged to be able to introduce Monica and Manny to these dignitaries. But the conflicts and contention that caused the January 6 attacks were far from finished.

On Tuesday, December 6, 2022, Pelosi invited me back to the Capitol, where our department was presented with a gold medal at the Rotunda. Right before the function began, a member of the Metropolitan Police heckled Michael Fanone, who cursed back at him. When Michael recently resigned after twenty years as a policeman, he'd excoriated everyone who'd downplayed the insurrection, to the chagrin of commanders and some fellow officers.

When it was over, Mitch McConnell and House Republican leader Kevin McCarthy went to shake the hands of the family of Brian

Sicknick. But his mother, father, and brothers walked right by, leaving McConnell and McCarthy with their hands extended.

"Good for them," Monica said.

I wasn't in that greeting line, but I was glad they did what I'd wanted to do. Politicians who were just paying lip service to our sacrifices did not deserve the photo op.

SOMEONE RECENTLY TWEETED, "Reminder to outraged MAGA folks that Osama bin Liden did not fly any of the planes on 9/11, and yet we still held him responsible." That resonated with me, because two years after the January 6 insurrection, almost a thousand defendants had been charged with assaulting, resisting, or impeding officers, including ninety-six individuals accused of using a deadly or dangerous weapon, according to the U.S. Justice Department. But they were mostly ordinary citizens who'd blindly followed the misinformation spewed by the most powerful man in the world. Despite the courageous Committee's recommendation to prosecute Trump, as of this writing, not one person responsible for planning, instigating, or paying for January 6 has been arrested yet.

MY LAST CAPITOL tour felt redemptive as I guided real tourists who came to pay respects instead of the insurrectionists who'd invaded to cause damage.

"I saw you on TV. You were brave to do what you did," said an older woman who recognized me. "It must be hard for you to come back here."

It was, but citizens who offered support helped me replace the horrible flashbacks with better memories. I took it upon myself to show her and her group around but avoided the tunnel. At the Lower West Terrace entrance where I'd almost died, I took photos of splintered glass on the ground. The entrance should be part of the guided tour so Americans could understand what we'd faced.

"See these little square specks still here?" I pointed. "They're from January 6, when rioters smashed the doors and windows."

The Security division installed an ID card reader outside the building instead of putting up bars or steel reinforcement doors to stop another invasion. The structure needed improvements, but the Capitol Police Board seemed more concerned with aesthetics than the logistics of safety. They'd replaced the glass panes but left the doors the same so they could easily be broken into again.

"Why can't they upgrade the physical security of the building?" I asked January 6th Committee Chairman Bennie Thompson the last time I saw him.

"I don't know, Sergeant Gonell," he answered. "It's been two years. It's not because of lack of funds. The money is there. They have a blank check."

At least the majority of our population did not vote any Capitol invaders into positions of trust and authority on November 8, 2022. Yet it scared me that the party who propagated a big lie about the election being stolen and abetted the attack was back at the helm of Congress. In violation of the Constitution, which disqualifies elected officials from holding federal office if they have "engaged in insurrection or rebellion against the [United States], or given aid or comfort to the enemies thereof," Trump announced another bid for the presidency. Despite the Committee's recommendation that he be criminally prosecuted for inciting the insurrection, conspiracy to defraud America, making a false statement, and obstructing Congress, nobody seemed able to stop him from running for our highest office. At age seventy-six, he is allowed to go after his old job while my career was destroyed at forty-two because of him.

Bureaucracy and red tape were frustrating as I remained part-time on the force, awaiting approval of my disability claim. On restricted duty, I was in limbo for months on end. As a victim and witness, I gave testimony for the FBI, district attorneys, and federal courts prosecuting forty cases against the rioters. Several invaders received jail terms ranging from three to fifteen years. In court during sentencing, they pretended to be remorseful and begged for leniency, only to later excuse their behavior by claiming things like "I was just caught up in the moment" and "I let my emotions get the better of me."

I couldn't believe their lawyers attacked my character by saying I was exaggerating, seeking attention, or speaking out for financial gain. I would have traded this sad spotlight for having my health, full-time job, and security back any day.

One defense attorney even had the nerve to ask me, "Were you even at the tunnel that day at all?" despite videos showing the moment my rotator cuff was torn by her client violently pulling me into the crowd. When I contradicted her statement and told her the defendant was lying, the lawyer said, "Don't take it personal, Officer."

"It's sergeant," I snapped. "And how can I not? You attacked me, saying what I lived through isn't true," I argued before the judge. "You're not showing the whole clip. If you show it all, you'll see what your client, Kyle Fitzsimons, did to me." Fitzsimons—the rioter who'd worn a butcher coat—was found guilty of eleven charges. Aiding the prosecution of those who'd hurt me had become my job.

Instead of continuing on as a police lieutenant, a position I'd worked my whole life for, I received notice from the U.S. Office of Personnel Management that my application for disability payment under the Federal Employees Retirement System had been approved. My employment would soon be ending. I was just one of the 20 percent of Capitol Police officers who wound up leaving as a direct result of the attacks. My official last day of work was midnight, December 17, 2022. That week, I was asked to take one final photograph for my retirement

220

credentials. I hesitated to hand back my police ID and sign separation documents, overcome with grief at the tragic culmination of my police career.

But I was grateful to learn that Congressman Bennie Thompson wrote a letter to the U.S. Capitol Police chief arguing that I should still receive the lieutenant promotion. That way, I could retire with a higher rank. The request was forwarded to the Capitol Police Board. I haven't heard back.

Recently my son was given a school assignment to write about someone who gives you pride. Manny showed off the White House photographs we'd taken and told his class, "Although my father wasn't born in this country like me, he's an Iraq War veteran and a police officer who defended the Capitol from the rioters on January 6. He's my hero."

His words reminded me that I had no regrets. I was proud to be a public servant and defender of my country and my country's democracy, calling out injustice when I saw it. Working at the Capitol, a majestic place where history was made every day, changed me. I hope I lived up to its nobility and made a small difference. If I had the choice whether to do it all again, I would. For Grandpa Fillo, who told me to make America my home, and for my son, who'll grow up here, inheriting a better future in this land of freedom worth fighting for.

ACKNOWLEDGMENTS

First and foremost, I want to thank *Dios* for protecting me in my times of need.

I would also like to express my gratitude toward my coauthor Susan Shapiro for putting the most compelling fragments of my life together so eloquently. Early on she shared a writer's adage, saying, "'If you got the story, tell it. If you ain't got it, write it.' And you got the story." We've been blessed to work with a brilliant literary team: agents Meg Thompson and Samantha Wekstein and Counterpoint's Dan Smetanka, Dan López, Megan Fishmann, and Rachel Fershleiser.

I'm grateful to lawyers Ellis Levine, Mark Zaid, David Laufman, and Jeff Zeelander for their wise counsel; the many district attorneys, FBI investigators, and the army of online sleuths identifying my attackers; and Yvonne Bryant for assisting me in my pursuit of justice while keeping me sane.

I wouldn't be here without my medical team: Doctors Daniel Hampton, Richard Derner, Jennie Polizzi, and therapists Sheryl Johnson, Ki Park, and Ana Rivera. You put my broken self back together the best you could and never allowed me to give up hope.

To Olivia Troye for taking me under her wing, Jon Stewart and John Feal for fighting for veterans and first responders and getting legislation passed for our care and families, and Jennie Hill from the Wounded Blue for her peer support.

Immense gratitude to the U.S. Capitol Police for allowing me to be a public servant while witnessing history every day. All my Civil Disturbance Unit members from all the Divisions, I'm in awe of your bravery despite the odds against us. To all the officers who did what we signed up for and my supervisors who had our best interest at heart: Sean Gallagher for fighting on my behalf, Thomas Lloyd for being a great leader, Marvin Reid for being a friend and esteemed mentor. To my buddy Harry Dunn for inspiring me to get into some "good trouble."

In memory of officer and veteran Brian Sicknick, and my deepest sympathy to the families of all the officers who died as result of their courageous work on January 6, 2021.

Thanks to the MPD for literally rescuing our asses. Your mutual support was instrumental in turning the tide in our attempt to restore order. I feel lucky that Sergeant Boegner had my back and that Daniel Hodges, Michael Fanone, Robert Glover, and Ramey Kyle took charge in the tunnel while I was fighting at the front line—and to the rest of the officers that showed up and remain unknown.

I am indebted to Speaker Nancy Pelosi and the January 6th Committee members: Chairman Bennie Thompson and Representatives Jamie Raskin, Pete Aguilar, Elaine Luria, Stephanie Murphy, Adam Schiff, and Zoe Lofgren. Special thanks to Representatives Adam Kinzinger and Liz Cheney for being the only two Republican elected officials who had the courage to listen to what my colleagues and I witnessed at a great personal cost, even when it wasn't pleasant or politically convenient, and for putting their country above their party.

To my grandparents; parents Sabina and Jose; siblings Tony, Giovanny, Liliana, and Stephanie; and friends who reached out when I needed support. To Jaime Prendergast, my adopted dad and confidant, thank you for all your wisdom and generosity both in and out of the army.

Lastly, to my beloved wife, Monica, and our son, Emmanuel, who have gone through so much and continue to stand by me. You are the reason I've survived.

Aquilino A. Gonell,
Former U.S. Capitol Police Sergeant

AQUILINO GONELL is a Dominican immigrant, former U.S. Army soldier, and Iraq War veteran. For seventeen years, he was a United States Capitol Police officer and was one of four police officers who testified before the House Select Committee investigating the January 6 insurrection. He's been featured on ABC, CBS, CNN, Telemundo, Univision, and NPR, and in *The New York Times*, *The Washington Post*, and *El Diario*. He is a recipient of the Congressional Gold Medal and the Presidential Citizens Medal. You can follow him on X at @SergeantAqGo.

© Dan Brownstein

SUSAN SHAPIRO is an award-winning Jewish American journalist. She is the author or coauthor of the acclaimed nonfiction books *Unhooked* (a *New York Times* bestseller), *The Forgiveness Tour* (a Jewish Book Council pick), *The Bosnia List* (an Oprah Book of the Week, ASJA Award winner, and William Saroyan International Prize nonfiction finalist), and *World in Between* (a Notable Book for a Global Society). She writes for *The New York Times*, *New York* magazine, *The Wall Street Journal*, *The Washington Post*, and *Newsweek*, among other publications. Find out more at susanshapiro.net.